The Rule of the
Society of St. John the Evangelist

The Rule

∿ of the ∿

Society of St. John the Evangelist

North American Congregation

COWLEY PUBLICATIONS
Cambridge, Massachusetts

Library of Congress Cataloging-in-Publication Data:
Society of St. John the Evangelist.
  The rule of the Society of St. John the Evangelist : North American congregation.
     p.   cm.
  Includes bibliographical references.
  ISBN: 1-56101-132-0 (alk. paper)
  1. Society of St. John the Evangelist—Rules. I. Title.
BX5971.S58S63   1997
255'.83—dc21   97-19605
                                                                                    CIP

Scripture quotations are taken from the *New Revised Standard Version* of the Bible, © 1989 by the Division of Christian Education of the National Council of the Churches of Christ in the United States of America.

The cross on the cover is the cross of the brothers of the Society of St. John the Evangelist, designed by Charlotte Hallett.

Third Printing
This book was printed in Canada on recycled, acid-free paper.

COWLEY PUBLICATIONS
907 Massachusetts Avenue
Cambridge, Massachusetts 02139
800-225-1534 • www.cowley.org

Contents

Introduction

This book is the published edition of the Rule of life of the North American Congregation of the Society of St. John the Evangelist, a religious order of men within the Anglican Communion. Many people associate the idea of religious orders only with the Roman Catholic Church, which has the great majority of them, some numbering thousands of members. But the monastic, or religious life, is a much wider phenomenon. There are thousands of monks and nuns in the Eastern Orthodox churches, and since the middle of the twentieth century dozens of Protestant religious communities have sprung up, most of them in Europe, with members largely drawn from the Reformed and Lutheran churches. Ecumenical religious communities also exist, most notably the world-famous Community of Taizé, with its Protestant, Roman Catholic, and Anglican brothers.

The Anglican Communion, to which the Episcopal Church in the United States and the Anglican Church of Canada belong, has long had religious orders, communities of men and women bound together in prayer, ministry, and worship under the vows of poverty, celibacy, and obedience, or their equivalent. The Anglican religious communities are less widely known today because the total number of their membership is relatively small, around fifteen hundred men and women. Although the largest of the Anglican communities have never grown beyond several hundred members, they have exercised an influence much greater than their numbers would suggest. In North America there are about twenty-four religious communities, including the Order of the Holy Cross, the Order of St. Helena, the Community of St. John the Divine, the Society of St. Francis, and the Order of St. Benedict. As in the Roman Catholic Church, a number of our Anglican communities are coming to the end of their lifespan; however, new communities are also coming in being, most notably in the Anglican churches of Africa.

Anglican religious orders first sprang up in the 1840s as an expression of the Oxford Movement, a renewal of the Church that began in England and emphasized the catholic heritage of Anglicanism, the primacy of the life of prayer and spiritual discipline, and the call to minister to the poor. The communities that have come into being since then cover the full spectrum of religious life, from contemplative monastics living in enclosure to communities focused on ministry. The majority of Anglican communities occupy a position in the middle: living an ordered community life based on regular common prayer, while expressing the call to service in many different forms of ministry, such as evangelism, spiritual guidance and renewal, training for ministry, healing and support, and advocacy for the poor and marginalized.

The Society of St. John the Evangelist was the first stable religious community of men to be established in the Anglican Church after the Reformation; the foundation of women's communities had started some twenty years before. Our chief founder was Richard Meux Benson (1824-1915), a priest who was a Student (that is, a teaching fellow) of Christ Church, the largest of the colleges of the University of Oxford. Because the community was founded in the parish of Cowley on the eastern side of the city, where Father Benson was developing the parish life of a new urban area, the community became known as "the Cowley Fathers." This popular name unfortunately obscured the fact that the community has always consisted of lay as well as ordained men. The community soon established other houses in India and South Africa. Currently, the English Congregation of the Society has three houses, in London, Oxford, and Haywards Heath.

One of the three founding members of the Society, Fr. Charles Grafton, was a priest of the Episcopal Church, and other Americans, and later Canadians, joined the Society. In 1870 the community began work in America and eventually the Society on this side of the Atlantic gained autonomy from the English Congregation. American members opened a branch of the community in Japan which lasted for several decades, and for almost fifty years the Society had a separate province in Canada based in Bracebridge, Ontario. The closure of that house was followed by a merger, resulting in the North American Congregation.

Today the Society in North America has two houses, both in Massachusetts. Most of the brothers live in the monastery in Cambridge, which has its own retreat house, while a smaller team of brothers lives at Emery House, a rural retreat house on a hundred acres of grounds at West Newbury, about fifty miles north of Boston. The community is international in composition, with brothers from Canada, England, and Japan, as well as the United States, and in the course of their ministry some brothers travel widely in North America and abroad. The Society is officially recognized as a religious community of the Church by the Episcopal Church in the United States and the Anglican Church of Canada.

The brothers pursue a variety of ministries: providing hospitality, leading retreats, offering spiritual direction, writing, preaching, teaching prayer, and conducting workshops. Individual brothers work with persons with HIV/AIDS and in programs that support the poor, and Br. Thomas Shaw, SSJE is the Bishop of Massachusetts. Standing in continuity with an ancient tradition linking monastic communities and books, Cowley Publications is a ministry of the Society, publishing a wide range of books on prayer, theology, and spirituality for the international Anglican Communion, as well as others in the body of Christ. This ministry is committed to developing a new generation of writers whose books will encourage people to think and pray in new ways about the life of faith and the future.

Associated with the Society is the Fellowship of St. John. This fellowship unites several hundred lay and ordained friends of the community who look to it for inspiration, follow a rule of life in harmony with ours, and support the Society with their prayer, work, and gifts.

Although communities can flourish spontaneously and informally for a while, gathered under the leadership of charismatic founders or in response to an urgent purpose, the need soon arises for an instrument which will articulate the identity of the community, express its ruling values and ideals, and specify its practices. In the western Christian tradition every religious community that wants any kind of recognition by the Church is expected to have such a document, traditionally called a rule. The purpose of a rule is twofold: it enables the community to sustain its specific identity and focus through changes in leadership and the succession of generations, and it enables the Church to confirm and validate the vocation of the community and to hold it accountable.

The word "rule" has a legalistic ring in English; the original Latin word *regula* suggests not so much a code of legislation but a means of regulating and regularizing. A rule sustains identity by mandating the rhythms of worship, spiritual discipline, prayer and rest, work and ministry. It sets out the patterns by which authority is distributed and where accountability is expected. It delineates the bounds of the community and describes the processes of initiation. And it connects the practices and ideals of the particular community or order with the gospel and the Christian mystery.

There are a vast range of these rules in the western Christian tradition, of which the most celebrated is the Rule of St. Benedict from the sixth century. Its widespread adoption several centuries after Benedict's death secured for it an immense influence throughout western civilization. In the eastern Church distinct religious orders did not develop; rules for monks, such as that of St. Basil, are more like handbooks of ascetical teaching. Individual monasteries supplement these traditional sources of spiritual guidance with an additional constitution, called a *typikon*, that specifies the particular type or pattern of monastic life that is followed there.

It was not until almost twenty years after the founding of the Society in 1866 that its Rule of life, and the statutes which made up its formal constitution, were officially adopted. Father Benson, its chief founder and first Superior, clearly had earlier versions which he expounded in his formative teaching of the first generation of members. The first official version, in which other members also had a hand, was subject to a number of minor revisions in the succeeding decades. When in 1935 the Society published "The Religious Vocation," a series of expository addresses on the main chapters of the Rule originally delivered in 1874, it was a later version of the Rule which was incorporated into the text.

The SSJE Rule was a short but formidable document. To some it seemed that Father Benson had succeeded in fusing the most demanding elements from a wide range of traditions. The Rule gave rise to a number of awed evaluations typified in the quip that the members of the Society were expected to be "Trappists at home and Jesuits abroad." In other words, it made normative an ascetic and monastic regimen of terrific austerity while mandating the detachment and mobility of those who were expected to be available for a wide variety of forms of mission. Although it contained some remarkable distillations of Father Benson's spiritual teaching, the document itself concentrates on setting very demanding standards of personal and collective austerity, gravity, and spiritual concentration.

In practice the Society seems to have found more inspiration in the teaching of Father Benson than in the actual Rule. We possess a large number of the addresses and meditations he gave to the community in its formative years, as well as the many books that he published, and it is these that demonstrate the depth and range of his insight and genius. Four volumes of his instructions on the religious life have been published by the Society.

The mid-1960s were a time of questioning and renewal for religious communities everywhere, largely under the influence of the Second Vatican Council. The Society's own changes were fairly cautious at that time, but it became obvious that it was necessary to update the Rule of life. At the end of that decade the entire Society adopted a revised version which was mainly the work of the Superior of the English Congregation. The revision was a conservative one which abbreviated the Rule by removing much secondary material. The result was a collection of very brief chapters in which the core of the original remained, though mellowed and modified in the light of modern concerns.

In the early 1970s under the leadership of the Superior, Br. Paul Wessinger, the American Congregation of the Society of St. John the Evangelist undertook the renewal of its life and ministry. This renewal gained fresh impetus in the 1980s under the dynamic leadership of his successor, Br. Thomas Shaw. In 1984 a merger with the Canadian Congregation resulted in a community that spanned the Episcopal Church and the Anglican Church of Canada. By the mid-1980s the changes and developments that were taking place in our ministry and way of life meant that the existing Rule no longer gave a true reflection of many aspects of the real life of the community. The Society came to a common mind that the Spirit was calling us to replace it.

The chief defect of the Rule was that it did not address a whole host of issues that we knew to be vital for the health and faithfulness of a community making the transition into the third millennium. We came to see that we needed a Rule which would be far more ample in its teaching about the specific identity of the Society and which would help us to hold ourselves accountable in many areas about which the former Rule was completely silent. We had no difficulty in recognizing that it was impossible merely to patch up the old Rule with new material, so we had to face the challenge of creating an entirely fresh document. And because the English branch of the community was in a very different situation from our own, the responsibility for this endeavor lay with us.

The call that we felt at that time was a daunting one. We knew that the renewal of the recent decade was not complete, yet we believed that it was precisely the prolonged and demanding process of collective creativity required to develop a new Rule that would further advance and deepen our renewal. In the actual struggle to articulate the community's vision and the covenant by which we live, we would grow closer together in Christ and come to know as a body how we are called to live.

We decided not to depend on studying the rules of other contemporary communities lest we short-circuit our own creative endeavor. We also made the apparently drastic decision not to refer directly to previous versions of the SSJE Rule. Far from representing a revolutionary intention to overthrow the tradition, this decision was an expression of confidence in the living continuity of tradition. We knew that the charism of the Society and the spiritual teaching of our past leaders was in our blood. We were convinced that authentic continuity would not consist in carrying over excerpts from the old Rule, but in our inner appropriation of the tradition and its rearticulation. While we distanced ourselves from the direct influence of the old Rule itself, we felt entirely free to draw on the wide range of the teaching of our forebears, in particular the writings of Father Benson.

Thus the Rule published here is a contemporary one, created by the Society of St. John the Evangelist over a period of eight years and formally adopted in September, 1996. A separate set of statutes, not printed here, governs the formal and legal aspects of its constitution. Our Society follows an ancient practice of reading a portion of the Rule aloud almost every day. We do so at a brief gathering for worship, called the Chapter Office, that ends the morning silence and begins the working day. The Rule is divided into short sections appropriate to this practice of reading aloud. Listening to the Rule being read helps us to experience it as a living word to us, rather than a document to be kept in a drawer.

The Society has adopted this Rule as an authentic expression of our life for today. We do not pretend that it will be adequate twenty or even ten years from now. Our life goes forward sustained by a deep conviction that we will continue to be challenged by the Holy Spirit to grow and change. We assume that as we continue to develop, our response to new challenges will give rise to significant revisions; even now we can begin to guess what some of these might be.

Change is overwhelming society and the Church at an unprecedented rate, and it is easy to become paralyzed by the sense that everything has become provisional, that nothing can really be decided or chosen. We have no idea what the future holds for religious communities. Though we ourselves are blessed with new members, many communities are no longer attracting people to them. A community like ours could be tempted to prolong the process of coming to a mind about the meaning and practice of our life indefinitely, holding ourselves open to further insights that might be just round the corner. We are glad to have received the gift from God of a sense of closure in our creative endeavor. We now go ahead with our life and mission confident in the standard that the

Rule now holds up to us, and equally confident that the community will be able to discern when it is time to begin again a special process of reevaluation.

Our sole motive in creating a new Rule of life was to strengthen our own community and our awareness of the particular vocation that God has given us; in other words, we produced it specifically for ourselves. Nevertheless, as we talked about our work on the Rule with individuals and other religious communities, we gradually became aware that our Rule might be of interest and useful outside the Society. By the time the work was largely completed many people had urged us to make the Rule available not only to our friends and other religious communities, but to a wider public by means of a published edition.

So we decided to offer this very intimate text that reveals the vision, prayer, and work of our community for meditation by those who already know us and who are seeking a deeper understanding of a way of life to which they feel attuned. And we offer it for those who do not know us yet, but who, in this time of widespread spiritual hunger when the monastic way is exerting a considerable pull on people's imagination and interest, seek a window into the life of a contemporary religious community.

Reflecting on these requests to have our Rule available and on our own sense of the value it might have for a wider readership, the community has come to see a number of compelling reasons for publishing it. In the first place, there are few rules of religious communities readily available to the general public: only the Rule of St. Benedict is published widely. The ecumenical Taizé Community, the Order of the Holy Cross, and the modern monastic Jerusalem Community have published their rules of life, but copies are often limited and hard to find. The publication of our own Rule will provide a means for the general reader to grasp more vividly and realistically how a religious community actually lives. Traditionally, most religious communities, except for those following an ancient rule, have kept their rule as a private document. We are opening our Rule to a wider readership to help make the religious life become more easily known and understood, particularly in the Episcopal Church and the Anglican Church of Canada.

Secondly, we offer the Rule as one example of renewal in the religious life. The rules of many religious communities have become antiquated, no longer authentic or adequate as expressions of contemporary religious life. Communities have several options in relation to their original rules. Some simply allow their original rule to stand, while freely adapting them in practice and welcoming new influences and values; others edit and modify their original rule. Some communities set aside their original rule entirely and replace it with a contemporary statement of gospel values and general principles, relying on a collection of statutes to spell out the basic ground rules of community life.

Our community has chosen a course of action that is both definitely traditional and also innovative. We decided that instead of living by a rule reduced to general principles, we would compose a new document that was not only thoroughly theological in its statements of belief and delineation of our common vision, but also very precise in spelling out the practices for which we hold one another accountable. Composing a rule is a very traditional thing to do; what is innovative is the freedom we have enjoyed in bringing into the Rule many themes that belong to our contemporary religious experience. We hope that our integration of contemporary insights about authority and responsibility, intimacy and sexuality, health and creativity, old age and death will be a source of encouragement for others who are committed to the renewal of religious life and spirituality.

Thirdly, we have been encouraged to believe that our Rule of life might serve as a model for other kinds of Christian groups who want to produce a comparable expression of their vision, life, and practice. A more detailed account of the actual process we used to create the new Rule is provided at the end of this book for the benefit of those who may be interested in knowing more about the way the community works together, and for members of communities who may be considering a similar project.

Finally, we believe that the Rule can be a source of rich inspiration for individual Christians who are prepared to meditate on its teachings. Following the text of the Rule we offer some guidelines to groups and individuals that we hope will help them make the fullest use of the inspiration the Rule has to offer.

THE RULE

ONE

The Call of the Society

God so loved the world that he gave his only Son, the eternal Word by whom all things were created, to become flesh and live among us. In all the signs that he did and the teaching that he gave, he made known to us the grace and truth of the eternal Father. When his hour came the Son consummated his obedience to the Father, and expressed his love for us to the uttermost, by offering himself on the cross. He was lifted up from the earth in his crucifixion and resurrection from the dead in order to draw all people to himself.

We whom God calls into this Society have been drawn into union with Christ by the power of his cross and resurrection; we have been reborn in him by water and the Spirit. God chooses us from varied places and backgrounds to become a company of friends, spending our whole life abiding in him and giving ourselves up to the attraction of his glory. Our community was called into being by God so that we may be entirely consecrated to him and through our common experience of the glory of the Father and the Son begin to attain even now the unity that God desires for all humankind. "The glory that you have given me I have given them, so that they may be one, as we are one, I in them and you in me, that they may become completely one, so that the world may know that you have sent me and have loved them even as you have loved me."

Our mission is inseparable from our call to live in union with God in prayer, worship, and mutual love. Christ breathes his Spirit into us to be the one source of our own conversion and of our witness and mission to others; "As the Father has sent me, so I send you." We are sent to be servants of God's children and ministers of the reconciliation which the Lamb of God has accomplished. Our own unity is given to be a sign that will draw others to have faith in him. Christ has entrusted to us the same word that the Father gave to him, so that those who hear it from our lips and perceive it in our lives may receive the light and through believing have life in his name.

By giving us the grace and courage to make lifelong vows of poverty, celibacy, and obedience in an enduring fellowship, God makes us a sign of his eternal faithfulness. A community of men who pledge to stay together until death is a powerful sign to the world of the grace that enables those who love Christ to abide until he comes.

The divine Wind that blows where it chooses has not restricted our Society to a few ministries. Varied gifts within our brotherhood bear witness to the living power of Christ and extend his salvation. Though our gifts differ we share one call to be consecrated in truth, through the power of God's word and the grace renewed by feeding on Christ and drinking his life-blood in the Eucharist. As a sign of our identity God gives us all an affinity with the witness of the beloved disciple embodied in the gospel of John. We bear the name of St. John the Evangelist to show the Church what is the source of our inspiration and our joy.

TWO

Our Dedication to the Disciple Whom Jesus Loved

We hear God's living word in all the scriptures but the testimony of the disciple whom Jesus loved has special power for those whom God calls into this Society. It gives us joy to know that Jesus drew this man John to himself in order to enjoy the blessings of close friendship. We believe that through our religious vocation Jesus is drawing us also into the deepest intimacy with himself. We find a profound significance for our own lives in what the fourth gospel tells us of the beloved disciple's friendship with Jesus and his call to be a witness to the mystery of the incarnation.

This is the man whom Jesus wanted to have closest to his heart at the last supper. The image of the trusted friend lying close to the breast of Jesus is an icon of the relationship we enjoy with the Son of God through prayer. It is by being close to him that we are reunited with the Father, for Jesus is "God the only Son, who is close to the Father's heart." And contemplating the closeness of the disciple to Jesus at the supper can deepen our awareness that the communion we have with Christ in the Eucharist is no mere abstract idea but a real and growing bond of personal love.

The beloved disciple did not hide from the suffering of Christ at Golgotha but took his stand there with Mary. By being steadfast together at the cross, enduring all that others found unbearable, they remained in Jesus' love. If we abide in that perfect love shown on the cross we will receive the grace to face together all that we are tempted to run from in fear. Christ's gift of enduring love will be the heart of our life as a community, as it was in the new family which he called into being from the cross when he gave Mary and John to one another as mother and son.

Only love can understand what God gives and reveals through Jesus. The beloved disciple understood that the pouring out of water and blood from Jesus' side signified the giving of the Spirit. Love will open our eyes to the Spirit's power in the sacraments, in prayer, in action and service. He went into the empty tomb, and believed at once in the mystery of the resurrection. Love will make us men of faith who know God's power to bring life out of death. The beloved disciple recognized the Lord in the stranger by the shore. Love will expand our ability to know him in all persons, in all things, and in all places.

The beloved disciple lived on, faithful to Christ's call to "remain until I come." The years spent exploring the depths of the revelation in which he had taken part bore fruit in the great gospel which bears the name of John. We have taken this name to show that we too are Christ's friends and witnesses. Through us also many come to believe that Jesus is the Son of God, and through believing have life in his name.

THREE

Our Founders and the Grace of Tradition

Just as we believe that our Society had its origin in the response to God's creative call of our founders, Richard Meux Benson, Charles Chapman Grafton, and Simeon Wilberforce O'Neill, so we believe that it is sustained through our own obedience to the voice of God continually calling us on. God speaks to us in many ways to maintain and renew the vocation of the Society. God speaks to us through the scriptures and the Christian tradition, through men and women of the Spirit of different ages and cultures, through our own experience, and through contemporary voices that engage us with the challenges of our own time.

Among the many voices that mediate God's call to us, the witness of our founders and predecessors in the Society has a special importance. God calls us to remember them and to value their testimony. Reflection on our community's own tradition, and a dialogue between our contemporary experience and that of our predecessors, helps us to sustain our identity as we strive to rise up to the demands of the present. As we explore the spiritual legacy of our forebears we remember that they are not dead figures from the past. Risen in Christ, they belong to the great cloud of witnesses who spur us on by their prayers to change and mature in response to the Holy Spirit who makes all things new.

Faithfulness to tradition does not mean mere perpetuation or copying of ways from the past but a creative recovery of the past as a source of inspiration and guidance in our faithfulness to God's future, the coming reign of God. As we meditate on the grace of tradition each of us will hear the call to become, in Father Benson's words, "a man—not simply of the day, but a man of the moment, a man precisely up to the mark of the times. This makes the religious—so far from being the traditional imitator of bygone days—most especially a man of the present moment and its life."

Our Society was the first religious community of men to be firmly established in the Anglican Church since the Reformation and embraced from the beginning both the contemplative and active dimensions of the religious vocation. As we struggle with God's call to us today to be active in ministry, prophecy, teaching, and service, and to have a deep life of prayer and worship, we shall find encouragement in remembering the example of our forebears in their dedication to the mystical and apostolic aspects of our calling.

There are many aspects to the witness of those who formed our Society's tradition. Their lives inspire us to be indifferent to celebrity and success and to trust the power of hidden prayer. They spur us to be prophetic critics of Christendom and its compromises and to be dedicated to the renewal of the Church. They summon us to have a world-wide vision of mission, to be adaptable to a wide variety of settings, to be available in ministry to all classes of people. They teach us to integrate the catholic and evangelical traditions and to dedicate ourselves to the ministry of reconciliation and unity.

Inevitably, the Society's past is also marred by many failures. God will have much to teach us through them, as long as we humbly keep in mind our own biases and shortcomings.

FOUR

The Witness of Life in Community

God has called us into being as a community and our life as a community, though fraught with struggles and failures, is a powerful act of revelation, testimony, and service. In community we bear witness to the social nature of human life as willed by our Creator. Human beings bear the image of the triune God and are not meant to be separate and isolated. All of us are called by God to belong to communities of personal cooperation and interdependence which strive to nurture and use the gifts of each and to see that our basic needs are met. Jesus called his disciples to be the light of the world, a city set on a hill which cannot be hid; through the vitality of our life as a community we are meant to help people remember their own calling to form community. In an era of fragmentation and the breakdown of family and community, our Society, though small, can be a beacon drawing people to live in communion.

One of the ways in which we promote community is by being the nucleus for a wider fellowship. This is formed through the relationships we establish in our varied ministries, especially the hospitality of our houses; through the Fellowship of St. John, whose members keep a rule of life in harmony with ours; by the participation of our personal friends and families; and by our neighbors regularly joining us in worship. Our proclamation of the good news is also an invitation to be in communion with us. "We declare to you what we have seen and heard so that you also may have fellowship with us." This wider family is a true expression of community sustained by many energies of mutual service. We not only serve our brothers and sisters by acting as a spiritual center and home and ministering to them; they support us in innumerable ways in prayer, through their gifts and voluntary labors, by teaching and inspiring us, and by working together with us in Christ. Some who find themselves relegated by neglect and prejudice to the margins of society will find a special grace in participating in this wider fellowship around our community.

Our human vocation to live in communion and mutuality is rooted in our creation in God's image and likeness. The very being of God is community; the Father, Son, and Spirit are One in reciprocal self-giving and love. The mystery of God as Trinity is one that only those living in personal communion can understand by experience. Through our common life we can begin to grasp that there is a transcendent unity that allows mutual affirmation of our distinctness as persons. Through prayer we can see that this flows from the Triune life of God. If we are true to our calling as a community, our Society will be a revelation of God.

Our life as a community should also be a sign to the Church to rise up to its true calling as a communion of the Holy Spirit, the Body of Christ and the company of Christ's friends. We are not called to be a separate elite, but to exemplify the life of the Body of Christ in which every member has a particular gift of the Spirit for ministry and shares an equal dignity. Father Benson taught that "there are special gifts of God indeed to the Society, but only as it is a society within the Church. The small body is to realize and intensify the gifts, to realize the energies, belonging to the whole Church." Our witness and ministry is not merely to separate individuals; it is for strengthening the common life in the Body of Christ.

FIVE

The Challenges of Life in Community

Every Christian is called to live in community as a member of the Church. Christ in his wisdom draws each disciple into that particular expression of community which will be the best means of his or her conversion. Our way of life in this religious community is one of many expressions of the common life in the Body of Christ. We can be confident that Christ has called us into our Society because he knows that the challenges and the gifts it offers are the very ones we need for the working out of our salvation.

The first challenge of community life is to accept wholeheartedly the authority of Christ to call whom he will. Our community is not formed by the natural attraction of like-minded people. We are given to one another by Christ and he calls us to accept one another as we are. By abiding in him we can unite in a mutual love which goes deeper than personal attraction. Mutual acceptance and love call us to value our differences of background, temperament, gifts, personality, and style. Only when we recognize them as sources of vitality are we able to let go of competitiveness and jealousy. As we actively seek to grow, and discern which men are being called into our Society, we must ardently seek for signs that God desires to increase our diversity in culture and race.

We are also called to accept with compassion and humility the particular fragility, complexity, and incompleteness of each brother. Our diversity and our brokenness mean that tensions and friction are inevitably woven into the fabric of everyday life. They are not to be regarded as signs of failure. Christ uses them for our conversion as we grow in mutual forbearance and learn to let go of the pride that drives us to control and reform our brothers on our own terms.

The Society's dedication to the fourth gospel draws us to see reflected in it certain values which we especially take to heart as we live in community. In John's gospel the community of disciples is portrayed as a circle of Christ's friends, abiding in him in obedience and love, and depending on the Advocate who leads them together into the truth. In this portrait we recognize an implicit critique of the tendency for communities to harden into institutions, and for officialdom to replace the spontaneity of mutual service. Our faithfulness to our calling will be seen in the ways in which we fearlessly subject our life to hard questions in the light of the gospel, resist inertia and rigidity, minister to one another generously as equals, and stay open to the fresh inspiration of the Spirit.

Because community life provides so completely for all our basic needs we must rise to the challenge of making sure that our sense of personal responsibility stays strong. Community life is arduous, and not an escape from the toil of earning a living. It is essential that work is distributed in such a way that each brother shares in its demands to the full extent of his ability. We are called to maintain an ethos that stimulates each of us to learn new skills by which he can serve the brotherhood and develop his ministry to others.

SIX

The Spirit of Poverty

The poverty we embrace through our vow has its source, supreme example, and eternal home in the being of God, who is a Trinity of Persons. In the Godhead there is no possessiveness, no holding back of self. Father, Son, and Holy Spirit are One in mutual self-giving and receiving. Faith sees the cross of suffering and self-giving love planted in the very being of the God revealed to us in Jesus. When God made room for the existence of space and time and shaped a world filled with glory, this act of creation was one of pure self-emptying. But God broke all the limits of generosity in the incarnation of the Son for our sake, "who, though he was in the form of God, did not regard equality with God as something to be exploited, but emptied himself, taking the form of a slave, being born in human likeness. And being found in human form, he humbled himself and became obedient to the point of death—even death on a cross." By the vow of poverty we bind ourselves to have "the same mind...that was in Christ Jesus."

The poverty that comes from God is not a barren emptiness. Christ "became poor, so that by his poverty [we] might become rich." It is only because we are being "filled with all the fullness of God" that we can pledge together in this shared vow to give ourselves away in a common life of worship, hospitality, evangelism, and service. "From his fullness we have all received, grace upon grace."

By this vow we renounce personal ownership. We are to be of one heart and soul, holding all things in common. By sharing everything we will be in harmony with the very being of God whose Triune life is boundless sharing. We will have a foretaste of the life of the communion of saints. We will recognize that the concern with individualistic fulfillment and private security that prevails in our culture is a trap from which we are being set free. More and more we will come to know that we were all baptized into Christ to be set free from self-centeredness. Our fulfillment comes together as members of one Body, and the Spirit will summon us again and again to surrender individual desires for the sake of our brotherhood and our mission.

If our religious poverty is to be authentic we must stay soberly aware of the essential difference between the deprivation of those whose poverty is forced upon them, and the way of life we choose by vow. We continue to be privileged by our education, our access to power, and our material security. Nevertheless, the Spirit has many ways of making us poor and we are in no doubt that they will be costly to accept. In particular we can be sure that the Society's life will be marked by fragility and many frustrating limitations. The resources to meet the demands made on us will seem inadequate, and our numbers too few. Our energies will seem insufficient for the claims made on them, and the task of balancing our life and husbanding our strengths too difficult. Even some of our ideals and dreams will need to be surrendered; the way God actually calls us to live may seem less appealing or less heroic than other forms of the religious life. God will give us our poverty. Every day we will be called to grow in reliance on grace alone and to surrender those inner and outer riches that hold us back from risking all for Christ, who risked and gave all for us.

SEVEN

Poverty and Stewardship in Practice

As we come to enter more completely into the offering of the Eucharist we learn more and more to offer thanks at all times and in all places. This gift of overflowing gratitude to God, who supplies all our needs, enables us to let go of dependence on possessions and all that is superfluous. In the sacrifice of thanksgiving lies the secret of simplicity of life to which we bind ourselves in the vow of poverty.

This simplicity of life finds expression in the way we enjoy and value the goodness of ordinary things and the beauty of creation. As we cherish the essential gifts of life, we grow in freedom from the compulsion to accumulate things, and cease to long for wealth. The movement towards simplicity puts us at odds with our culture, which defines human beings primarily as consumers, and gives prestige to those who have the power to indulge themselves in luxury and waste. As a community and as individuals we shall have to struggle continually to resist the pressure to conform. Our vow of poverty inevitably commits us to conscientious participation in the movement to establish just stewardship of the environment and earth's resources.

Our personal responsibility in this vow means taking care to gather around ourselves only what is appropriate and necessary. We must always seek the permission of the Superior to keep any gifts offered to us. We shall readily share among ourselves the things we have for our use, and give away whatever we cease to need. Whenever we have reason to buy anything for our own use we are to be watchful for temptations to be irresponsible. Our collective responsibility involves us all in the careful stewardship of our resources, especially in the policies which govern the use of our endowment and properties. Those who have responsibility for using funds allocated by the community need to guard against the temptation to misuse this power by spending thoughtlessly or failing to involve others in significant decisions.

The security we enjoy as a community makes us strangers to the precariousness and destitution that are the lot of the poor. Therefore we come to the poor in need of their witness to what it means to be powerless and to put one's trust entirely in God. As a community we must continually watch for signs that God is calling us to live and work with those who endure the hardships of material poverty. Even when our work among God's poor is limited in scope we should be their allies in every way. Our vow binds us to ruthless self-examination as to our real solidarity with the poor. In our education, preaching, and political lives we are committed to advocacy for the poor, and the struggle to restore to them their just share of power and the bounty of God.

EIGHT

Engaging with Poverty

The vow of poverty is a commitment of faithfulness to the gospel itself which summons us to a new vision and way of life which reverse the values of the world. The beatitudes of Jesus call us to trust the promise of divine fulfillment hidden in things that the world counts as barren and negative. By our vow we reaffirm our baptismal renunciations and pledge ourselves to seek out the mystery of divine grace present in places and experiences which seem insignificant, dark, or empty.

By our vow of poverty we recognize that in our own spiritual lives there will be seasons in the shadow, experiences of dryness, waiting, obscurity, and the seeming absence of God. In the light of the gospel we know that these are necessary, and that some of them yield more blessings than times when we are filled with devotion and confidence. "Every branch that bears fruit he prunes to make it bear more fruit." Our whole spirituality should bear the mark of our vow, showing that God is freeing us from dependence on feelings of success and happiness.

Poverty involves radical truthfulness about our own persons and the community itself, grounded in the knowledge of our fallibility and brokenness. Popularity and acclaim are dangerous as they can lure us away from that sober awareness of our spiritual poverty which compels us to confess that "this extraordinary power belongs to God and does not come from us." The knowledge and acceptance of our fragility preserves us from complacency and illusion, continually throwing us back on the mercy and compassion of God.

In the great prayer of Jesus in the fourth gospel he says of his disciples, "They do not belong to the world, just as I do not belong to the world." The vow of poverty is one of the chief ways in which we affirm our separation in Christ from everything in the world that opposes God's way of self-spending love. It sets us in opposition to ways of coercion, violence, and militarism. It commits us to reject in Christ's name every manifestation of exploitation, prejudice, and oppression. It calls us to dissociate ourselves from structures of privilege and wealth. By this vow we confess the rule of the cross: "God chose what is foolish in the world to shame the wise; God chose what is weak in the world to shame the strong; God chose what is low and despised in the world, things that are not, to reduce to nothing things that are." Through the vow of poverty we pledge ourselves to look for the signs of God's activity and glory, especially in the lives of those who are strangers to success and power as the world defines them.

One of the signs that our poverty is authentic will be the readiness of others to confide in us their own experiences of suffering, grief, and loss. If we are evading the mystery of poverty in our own lives we will shut ourselves off from the pain and weakness in the lives of our brothers and sisters. If we are living our vow they will find in our company a holy place of acceptance and understanding, where they can wait for God to bring strength out of weakness and resurrection from death.

NINE

The Vow of Celibacy

Through our vow of celibacy we offer ourselves as members of a community to be completely available to Christ. We commit ourselves to remaining single forever, instead of united to another in marriage or partnership. We pledge to forego the expression of love through sex, which God has blessed as the means for human partners to become one.

It is our desire to make a vow of celibacy that is the deepest possible expression of trust in Christ, who has chosen us to follow this path. Christ is the creative Wisdom through whom the Father created all things; he is the Light who lightens all who come into the world. Our sexuality, our power to love, our creative energy for relationship and union are of his making. They reflect the mystery of the triune life and mirror God's passionate love for all creation. In our vow we offer these gifts that belong to the heart of our humanity to Christ, trusting that he will bless, shape, and use them. Our faith in Christ as creator also expresses itself by revering our manhood itself as sacred. If we foster a climate of celibacy in which this faith and reverence flourish, each brother, whatever his sexual orientation, can come to accept fully the particular way the mystery of sexuality has been woven into the texture of his humanity.

Our vow is also a response to Jesus' own way of life. His own freedom from ties of family and home, in order to be completely available in the Spirit for the proclamation of the good news, attracted others to choose the same path. They trusted in his promise that their choice, though full of painful losses and risks, would bring the reward of an abundance of new relationships among those who were awakening to the joy of the Kingdom: "a hundredfold now in this age—houses, brothers and sisters, mothers and children...and in the age to come eternal life." When we make our vow we affirm our own confidence in this promise.

We make our vow also trusting in the healing power of Christ, the redeemer of human brokenness. Our capacity for intimacy, our sexual desires, our readiness to be faithful, are all damaged by the confusions and wounds of our fallen human condition. For us celibacy is a path of healing and redemption, as the vocation of marriage and partnership is for others. As we make our vow we acknowledge humbly our need for grace to give us that unity and integrity of heart which we can never attain by our own power. We set out on the celibate way as a path of salvation that gives us the hope of attaining maturity as loving, disciplined, and free men.

Our vow flows also from the experience of Christ, ascended and glorified, dwelling in our own hearts. Though we have surrendered the fulfillment we may have found in marriage or partnership, the mystery of union and mutual love is truly given to us. In the emptiness and absence that celibacy opens up in our hearts, Christ waits to make known to us the infinite strength and tenderness of his love. The exploration of our sexual solitude through prayer will reveal the depth of Christ's desire to be the one joy of our hearts. We can find the joy of celibacy only by entering into the mystery of our union with him and returning his love.

TEN

Celibate Life

Each of us will pass through different phases in our lives of celibate chastity. At times we will be glad of our inner solitude, which fosters prayer, and the diversity of relationships we enjoy in community and with friends; at other times we will feel loneliness. While others are enjoying the consolations of community life, some brothers may be missing the solace of partnership, the joys of sex, and the satisfaction of having a home of their own. There will be seasons of contentment in our singleness; there may be days of testing and confusion if we fall in love, or become strongly attracted to another. Struggles will come at different stages as we break through to new levels of integration; the challenges faced by young religious will not be the same as those that come with the onset of middle age. Old age may bring its own trials of doubt. Only if we share these different experiences in candor and trust can we offer one another genuine support.

At times many of us will miss having fathered children. We shall need to open the poignancy of this loss to Christ in prayer. He will show us that in union with him our lives have been far from barren. As we nurture others in Christ, and bring them to maturity, we shall discover that fatherhood has found expression in our lives. In prayer, meditation, our thought, our work, and our friendships, we are called to fulfill our deep human urge to be creators with God of new life, and to bear fruit that lasts.

The disciplines that let chastity take root in our lives are not mere curbs. Their purpose is to help us live with vitality and spirit. When we meditate we should truly pray with our bodies, and dwell on the glory with which the indwelling Spirit endows them. We are to reverence our bodies and do justice to their need for regular exercise and adequate sleep. Physical sloth and stress from overwork are equally liable to make sexual tension worse. Lethargy makes us more susceptible to the escapism of fantasy.

The disciplines that foster celibacy include those which prevent our spirits from becoming solemn and heavy. We can all contribute to the sanity and balance of our life together by allowing playfulness and humor to keep us in touch with our humanity and to release tension.

Jesus taught chastity of the heart, not merely of outward behavior. The conversion of our imaginations continues all our lives as we seek to make his integrity our own. We shall need to examine our hearts often to test the degree of our emotional honesty in our relations with others, and our faithfulness in honoring our personal boundaries. Whenever we are in perplexity or temptation it is essential to open our hearts to our spiritual directors or confessors; secrecy makes us more likely to deceive ourselves.

It is through friendship that we will be of most support to one another. Celibacy could be unbearably lonely unless we uphold one another with affection. Our friendship with one another does not draw us away from the centrality of the love of Christ in the heart, for that is the very thing we all have in common.

ELEVEN

The Witness of Celibacy

Our lives of committed celibacy can act as a powerful sign of the reality of God's grace. As we grow in our understanding of the meaning of our vow we are called to become more aware of our role as witnesses. The celibate life is a risky one. If it is lived as a cowardly way of avoiding intimacy and commitment, it can wither the soul. But if as celibates we embrace our sexuality as a divine gift, and draw upon it as a source of energy and creativity, we can bring hope and encouragement to many who meet us.

Our singleness of life awakens the need to discover within our own selves the mystery of the male and female dimensions of the divine image. If we are courageous in this exploration, and cooperate with the converting power of the Spirit, we can bear a significant witness to both men and women. Women will find encouragement if they encounter in us not only the security that comes with deep respect, but also empathy of soul. Men will find encouragement if they encounter in us confident forms of masculine identity that do not depend for their vigor on force or competition.

Our fidelity to this vow can be an encouragement to those who are united in the sacrament of Marriage; like them we depend on divine grace to help us remain steadfastly together until death, through all the changes and trials of life. Some partners of the same sex who have made a covenant of faithfulness in Christ may find inspiration in our loyalty and perseverance.

We are also witnesses to those who for many reasons live single lives. Much of the confusion and pain in fallen humanity's struggle with sexuality stems from the illusions that sexual activity is essential to wholeness, and that other forms of intimacy are inferior to the sexual bond. We can help people by the example of our lives to honor the depth and fullness to be found in the intimacy of friendship. We can bring inspiration and support to the struggles of those who seek to find meaning and purpose in their singleness. In our ministries, especially of hospitality, our celibacy gives us a special freedom to provide a setting in which single people of all ages and walks of life find respect, welcome, and affirmation.

TWELVE

The Spirit of Obedience

The Gospel of John will teach us to experience obedience as a growing freedom to love all that God desires and wills. Jesus bears witness to this freedom: "Very truly, I tell you, the Son can do nothing on his own, but only what he sees the Father doing; for whatever the Father does, the Son does likewise....My judgment is just, because I seek to do not my own will but the will of him who sent me." On our own we are powerless to act in selfless freedom in response to God's desire. Obedience is only possible because Christ dwells in us and we dwell in him through baptism. His obedience is active within us, drawing us into his union with the Father. By the vow of obedience we join together to make this loving consent to God's will the corporate offering of a community. We learn together to listen intently to God, and we support each other in the struggle against all that resists God within and around us.

The vow has many facets. It is a pledge to unite in a common response to God by embracing and fulfilling the Rule of the Society. It is a promise to work together to discern God's will as a body and act in concert to God's glory. The vow binds us to cooperate with the Superior in carrying out our mission. It is a pledge to listen to the voice of the Spirit speaking within the heart and to respond to God's invitations to self-surrender.

Resurrection into the freedom and constancy of Christ's obedience can be attained only through death and burial in union with him. Our share in humanity's sinfulness means that we are still hindered by fear of what God desires and resistance to what God ordains. As a community bound together in obedience we support one another through the inevitable pain of dying to our old selves, and encourage one another to trust in the goodness of God's will for us. The community is a school of reconciliation, conversion, and healing for sinners, in which we can grow in our capacity to give ourselves to God.

Obedience is also a path of detachment. We have our own ideas of how best to serve God, our dreams of serving in particular ways. God's actual call will often be to follow in other ways; as our vocation unfolds we will find that obedience requires us to lay aside again and again the plans we had made for ourselves. Monastic obedience gives us constant practice in letting go of attachment to our individual preferences and learning to trust in the wisdom of the community. It trains us to be resilient and prompt in responding to the Lord in the here and now.

The vow of obedience is fraught with risks. In the name of obedience human beings have gladly abdicated responsibility and taken refuge in passivity and conformity. Unless our obedience is in the Spirit we could be tempted to use the life of the community as a shelter from claiming and using our own responsibility and power as sons of God. The vow of obedience requires us to be constantly attentive to the voice of the Spirit within our hearts, endowing us with our own unique authority and gifts. We are called to be obedient to our true selves as they are being formed in Christ. Only where there is a growing respect for our true selves can there be authentic participation in the community's common endeavor to discern and carry out God's will.

THIRTEEN

Obedience in Practice

By the vow of obedience each brother gives his complete allegiance to the community by accepting the Rule of life as his own. The Rule is the expression of our distinctive way of discipleship. It embodies the values, disciplines, and patterns of response that experience has shown to sustain our identity. In the vow we promise to cherish the Rule as a gift, being attentive as we read it together and taking it to heart through meditation.

The vow is a pledge to put our whole heart into the community's continuous quest to learn the will of God for us and to do it. God has called us to be active co-creators in Christ, not passive recipients of external instructions. Obedience calls us to pray, to search our hearts and minds together, to consult and discuss with one another, to bring passion and commitment to our cooperation as brothers and ministers in the New Covenant. Our hope is to reach a common mind in our discernment and decisions as often as we can. When a brother disagrees with a decision that commends itself to most of us, the vow of obedience gives integrity to his subsequent support of the outcome.

Grace makes it possible for our obedience to one another to transcend mere acquiescence and to express instead the power of brotherly love and unity. In our cooperation with the Superior we should arrive through discussion at a full understanding of the response or task that is being proposed and pledge ourselves to full accountability. If difficulties occur in following through on any project we should promptly consult with him so that the goal can be realistically reset. We should observe the same standard of cooperation and accountability in our response to any brother who has been given authority in any sphere. In particular we are to give our full cooperation to the brother in charge of the house we live in.

We express our obedience also in the way we are receptive to the Superior's teaching and pastoral ministry, and the openness we have to one another's contributions to the common life.

The practice of obedience to our own interior wisdom as it is being inspired by the Spirit requires us to search our own desires and motives in prayer. In any case where our conscience seems to be in conflict with something required of us in community we should open our hearts to the Superior about it promptly. The vow encourages us to listen to our own hearts so that we can take responsibility for setting our own goals in the unfolding of our development as men of God. It requires us to be attentive to our own needs and gifts. It spurs us to be imaginative and hopeful about ourselves as active contributors to our common life.

If we remain alert we will see the signs that reveal whether we are indeed being converted. Where obedience is still immature there will be passivity, complaining, resentment, reluctance to be held accountable, rigidity, and lack of candor. Where obedience is emerging from a growing freedom we will recognize the fruits of the Spirit in frankness, initiative, generosity, and flexibility. We need to pray for these fruits not merely for our own good but so that our community can be a sign in the Church of what it means to be a living branch of the true vine.

FOURTEEN

The Office of Superior

The professed brothers elect one of their number who they believe has the necessary gifts of the Spirit to lead the Society. The community, faithful to our tradition and vocation that calls for strong leadership, entrusts authority to him which he exercises in these ways as the servant of all.

The Superior is empowered to distribute leadership and share administration throughout the community by choosing the officers and allocating specific areas of responsibility to the brothers. All the brothers are accountable to him in the exercise of their responsibilities. He coordinates the ministries of the community and no new work can be accepted without his permission. The Superior is also the chief pastor of the brethren and has the ultimate responsibility in Christ for the well-being of all. Although the Superior never acts as confessor within the community, and must honor the boundaries of each brother's inner life, if he is to serve and cherish the brothers he needs to know what is important in their lives. By fulfilling his share of the responsibility for staying genuinely in touch, each brother helps make sure that the Superior's ministry to him is timely and effective.

He is responsible for guiding the community as it makes plans and decisions. He presides over meetings of the Chapter in which important decisions are made by vote. He makes sure that less formal decisions are made with appropriate discussion and consultation. The Superior has the freedom to make various decisions about community policy on his own authority. The limits of this freedom are defined by the Statutes and maintained by the collective wisdom of the community. Once a year the community shall hold a discussion in which the Superior's ministry of leadership is reviewed.

The Superior serves the community as chief interpreter of the Rule. He is expected to enrich the community through his own spiritual teaching and by inviting men and women of the Spirit to give us guidance and inspiration. The Superior also receives a mandate to lead the community as a prophet who looks to the future and fosters our collective vision. This orientation towards God's future finds a particular expression in the way the Superior cultivates gifts of leadership within the community and equips potential successors. The Superior may not serve more than three consecutive terms of three years, to make sure that the gift of leadership is renewed.

The office of Superior needs outside resources of support. In addition to a spiritual director the Superior shall have regular recourse to a consultant of his choice who is qualified to help him monitor his ministry.

The benefits of endowing our leader with strong authority are great, but so are the demands. We need to be aware of both the negative and positive psychological forces that are inevitably brought into play wherever authority is strong. The Superior can be overwhelmed by the number of expectations placed upon him. He will not be equally gifted in meeting them all and will fall short through his own weakness. Only prayer and genuine love can sustain him in his office. The brothers shall frequently call upon God to give our leader the graces needed for his ministry day by day, and to show us how to support and cherish him.

FIFTEEN

Outward Signs of
Our Common Life

From the day of our clothing to the day of our burial, the habit acts as a powerful sign of our common life and identity that we should cherish. It manifests not only our membership in this Society but our solidarity with men and women following the monastic way the world over. It expresses a precious continuity linking us through the centuries to the beginning of the monastic movement in the Church of Christ.

This clothing, dense with meaning, is a source of joy. We have put on Christ in baptism and the habit can remind us of our present union with him. The triple-cord round our waists is an ancient sign of readiness that can summon us to be prepared to meet Christ whenever he should come. The knots tied in the cord at profession are signs to the hand and eye of the vows we have made to abide faithfully until he comes.

Each house of the Society shall have its own guidelines about when the habit will be worn at home. Sometimes when we are away on mission wearing our habits may be a valuable witness to our calling, but whenever the habit is likely to be a barrier in our dealings with others we should wear ordinary clothing. The habit loses its spiritual value if it is used for ostentation or to imply a false distinction between ourselves and other Christians.

The cross of the Society is an emblem of our common life to be worn with ordinary clothing whenever we choose. It enables us to bear close to our heart a sign of the lifting up of Christ from the earth that he might draw all people to himself.

When we make our life profession, we are given as a further sign of our entire dedication to Christ a ring to be worn thereafter at all times. This ring is a sign of our espousal as lovers of God. It shows our solidarity with those who have made vows to meet the demands of love and faithfulness in marriage and dedicated partnership.

It is a joyful thing to have our lives enriched by these and other symbols, but their power will fade if we fail to renew our appreciation of their depths. The occasions when a brother is given the habit and cross, or puts on the ring, are opportunities when we can all re-experience the richness of these symbols, and from time to time we should meditate on them in our prayer. Our hallowing of these outward signs involves taking care of them, particularly making sure that our habits are clean and in good repair.

SIXTEEN

Worship

Human beings were created to bless and adore their Creator and in the offering of worship to experience their highest joy and their deepest communion with one another. In our fallenness we continually turn in upon ourselves to seek fulfillment without self-offering. We squander on lesser things the love which is due to the one source of all being. But the Father never ceases from seeking true worshipers to worship him in spirit and truth. God sent the Son into the world to heal and raise us up so that, empowered by the Spirit, we could surrender our whole selves in adoration and be reunited in the love of God. God draws us into our Society so that our calling to be true worshipers can reach fulfillment in the offering of the continual sacrifice of praise. In this life of worship together we are transformed in body, soul, and spirit.

We offer our worship in the Spirit as a community of the Church on behalf of the entire world. Our life is ordered so that we can sustain the full expression of the Church's worship in the constant offering of the Daily Office and the Eucharist. We bear witness to the riches of the liturgy and its power to permeate life with the remembrance of God. Our liturgical life is in itself a vital ministry. We lift up the Church and world in prayer, and strengthen those whom we encourage to take full part in our worship. We also influence the renewal of the Church's worship by our example, and the value we place on beauty in music, dignity in ceremony, and depth in the word.

If we become the true worshipers whom the Father seeks, no part of our life is untouched by our worship. It makes our experience of time itself sacred. The offices express the inmost meaning of the times of each day from dawn to nightfall. The weeks are sanctified, beginning with the commemoration of the resurrection on the first day. The liturgical cycle of the year redeems the passage of time by making the months and seasons the means of appropriating again the creating and healing acts of God, reaching its climax in our renewed experience of the life-giving cross and resurrection in Holy Week, Easter, and Pentecost.

Our worship will bind us in community with one another and with those for whom we intercede in the liturgy. It unites us with our brothers who have gone before us and to the entire communion of saints. In worship we are not bound to our own time and place; the commemoration of the saints links us with all the ages and every place where God has been glorified. It reveals to us the great cloud of witnesses in the heavens, encouraging us on our straight course to God.

Worship sanctifies work, continually interrupting it so that we can offer it to God in thanksgiving. Worship, like play, is free from the need to produce tangible gains, but it is work. It takes skill to craft and carry out the "work of God," as monastic tradition calls it. Worship makes costly demands on our time and energies. It calls us from the inertia of self-centeredness. When we come to worship in dryness and fatigue, we learn to make the offering of sheer faith and allow ourselves to be borne along by the devotion of our brothers.

SEVENTEEN

The Eucharist

Our worship of God finds its fullest expression in the celebration of the Holy Eucharist. It is the offering through which we return thanks for all that God has given us in creation, and in our redemption through the pouring out of Christ's life-blood on the cross. In this sacrifice of bread and wine all that we do and are is joined by the Holy Spirit to the eternal offering of Christ on behalf of the world. It is the meal which intensifies our union with Christ, draws us together as a community, and nourishes us with the grace needed for our transformation and our mission. It is the mystery through which we are caught up into the communion of saints on earth and in heaven, the mystical Body of Christ. It is the gift through which we experience a foretaste of the life to come.

The celebration of the Eucharist on the first day of the week is our central act of worship as members of the people of God. Our seeking to abide in Christ and to feed on him constantly as our daily bread moves us to celebrate the Eucharist also on other days of the week. Although it is not our custom to offer the Eucharist on our day of rest, and there may be another day in the week at which participation is voluntary, the community will normally celebrate the Eucharist together day by day. Reservation of the sacramental gifts enables the community not only to communicate the sick, but also to have a sign of Christ's abiding presence in our midst.

John the Evangelist alludes to a profound dimension of the mystery of the Eucharist in the account of Jesus washing the feet of the disciples at the last supper. The Eucharist is a means for Christ to serve us and to give us the love whereby we can serve and love one another. Our celebrations of the Eucharist are occasions of spiritual hospitality, mutual service, and witness. Eucharistic hospitality is an important ministry to all those to whom we open our worship. We should be sensitive to their needs and order the liturgy in a welcoming way that enables them to participate with us. Through our celebrations we bear witness to our faith in the presence of the risen Christ in the living word of Scripture and preaching, in the assembled body, and in the sacramental Body and Blood of communion. Our eucharistic worship is a primary expression of our mission because it has the power to draw people into a living encounter with Christ, the living bread and true healer.

The frequent offering of the Eucharist is a privilege but it also brings challenges. We need to work together in revitalizing our eucharistic worship so that it does not become a repetitive routine. Creative variations in our liturgies are important. Frequent communion is a challenge to us also as individuals. It is not possible for us to participate in the liturgy with intense devotion and awareness every time. Often we must accept being borne along by the corporate devotion of the assembly, remembering that the power of the sacrament is not dependent on our mental clarity or warmth of feeling. However, each one of us will need to discover for himself ways of constantly renewing through meditation his self-offering and receptivity, so that we can come to communion often "with that tender love which is due to Him with whom we are so mysteriously united," as Father Benson urged us.

EIGHTEEN

The Daily Office

Each eucharistic meal empowers us to approach God afresh in worship, united with Christ; Father Benson teaches us that "just as in Holy Communion we receive His substance into our bodies, so in the saying of our offices we bring forth the power of that substance, so that it may rise up to God." The Daily Office is a sustained act of union with Christ by which we participate in his unceasing offering of love to the Father. In reciting the psalms, singing canticles and hymns, proclaiming the divine word in Scripture, or lifting our voices in prayer, we are to enter more and more into the mind, heart, and will of Christ, and to be borne up by the Spirit in him to the Father. Our praying of the psalter, which is the heart of the Daily Office, takes us ever deeper into the mystery of the incarnation; the psalms give voice to the whole range of human experience which Christ has embraced and redeemed as the Savior of the world. Although nothing essential is lacking when the office is said, we continue the tradition of our Society by singing whenever there are sufficient voices. As we sing and chant deep levels of our being are involved; our hearts are lifted up in greater exultation. And music enhances our worship with riches inherited from many ages.

This fellowship in praise at the heart of the Church continually deepens our integration as a community, making us one in Christ. Our desire to experience this deepening communion will find expression in the care we give to the disciplines of choral prayer. Among these disciplines are practice and preparation; the custom of taking our place in good time; stillness of posture; attentiveness to the readings; sensitivity and responsiveness to one another so that we can sing and recite together.

The office will also nourish the inner life of each brother. It is the means by which our hearts are constantly impregnated with the riches of the word of God in Scripture so that they bear fruit in our prayer and life. When a brother's heart is full of heaviness, praying the office can sustain him. But for the office to be truly a means of our transfiguration we must cooperate by continually renewing our inner attentiveness, laying aside again and again the preoccupations and daydreams which confuse and tie us down. This effort to keep our hearts open to Christ will be needed all our lives; it is a hidden dying to self day by day.

The Daily Office offered by the Society shall be drawn from *The Book of Common Prayer* of the Episcopal Church or of its equivalent in the Anglican Church of Canada: Morning Prayer, the Order of Service for Noonday, Evening Prayer, and Compline. Each house will establish a pattern in the recitation of the offices and the celebration of the Eucharist which best suits the local setting.

Each brother shall take part in every office unless he is permitted to be absent for reasons of infirmity or is prevented by some necessary work. We shall recite Morning and Evening Prayer by ourselves if we are unable to join the community in choir and when we are away from the house. In this way the community remains united in the common offering of praise even when we are separated.

NINETEEN

The Word of God in Preaching

Preaching is central to our full experience of the living presence and power of Christ in our worship. Although we do offer the Eucharist at certain times when silent reflection on the readings is judged to be sufficient, a homily will usually be preached at our regular community celebrations of the Eucharist. In preaching, Christ, who will be present to us in communion, comes first to those who are listening in "the word of God…living and active, sharper than any two-edged sword," and as the one who speaks words that "are spirit and life." The preached word is thus part of our experience of the daily bread of God's nourishment.

Certain brothers will be given by God a special gift of the Spirit for preaching, but the same Spirit distributes among the brothers the ability to share their experience of God and express their faith in the gospel through homilies offered at the Eucharist. Some brothers may participate in the preaching life only as listeners, but the formation that everyone coming into the community receives should enable most of us to preach. This exchange of the living word among us is a powerful expression of the communion of the Holy Spirit. In preaching we share with one another the fruits of our prayer, experience, and study and build up the common life. We learn to value one another's uniqueness as we come to appreciate our varied styles and distinctive approaches. We experience the mysterious action of the Spirit who sometimes touches our hearts with particular power when the words of the preacher are not in themselves especially eloquent or strong.

We shall need to renew our attentiveness to the preached word often. Openness will only be sustained if we ask for it, humbly confessing to God our tendency to be distracted. Courtesy and mutual respect encourage us to show through our posture and responsive attitude that we are listening to the preacher and not turning away from his offering. We need to let go of prejudices that deter us from being alert and ready for the gift that a brother might bring to us in his homily. In our prayer we are called to savor and meditate on the new gifts that have come to us through listening to one another's preaching so that they can be truly absorbed.

We will grow in our abilities as ministers of the word if we give and receive thoughtful responses to one another's preaching. Expressions of appreciation and thoughtful and sensitive criticism belong to that "speaking the truth in love" which builds up the body and makes our gifts more fruitful. At regular gatherings of the community time will be set aside for corporate reflection on our preaching.

Although we preach to one another as members of a community we must include the guests who worship with us; they are important members of our liturgical assembly. The word we preach is meant to address their claims and needs as well as our own, and the presence of different people from many walks of life is an incentive to keep before us wide spiritual horizons and challenging questions. People are hungry for good news that life is full of meaning in union with God. As we take turns to preach in the liturgy we remember our primary calling to be witnesses and messengers of that good news.

TWENTY

Holy Scripture

The life we live is permeated by Holy Scripture; it has a central place in our worship, our preaching, our meditation and reading, and our study. Through the scriptures the living voice of God is continually active to convert, nourish, and transform us. The more we open ourselves to their riches, the more we have to share with others. And the more we open the scriptures to others, the more we discover in them for our own lives.

In the Daily Office and the eucharistic liturgy of the word Scripture is continually absorbed into our beings, as we pray the psalter and canticles and listen to the readings and preaching. In our worship the Spirit sometimes touches us immediately through a word, an image, or a story; there and then we experience the Lord speaking to us. But we shall often go unaware of the ways in which the images and words of Scripture are seeping into the deepest level of our hearts. These hearts of ours are not empty vessels but inner worlds alive with images, memories, experiences, and desires. It is the Spirit dwelling within us who brings the revelation of Scripture into a vital encounter with our inmost selves, and brings to birth new meaning and life. Gradually we become aware of the deep resources of truth that this inner process of revelation has formed in us, and are able to draw upon them for our own needs and for the building up of others in ministry. The effect of the scriptures upon us in the liturgy is largely subliminal but this fact does not justify inattentiveness. We should take care to read the scriptures with a clarity and energy which does justice to our love for them, and to listen as attentively as we can.

In our personal lives of prayer we shall feed on the scriptures and trust in expectant faith that God will be present in them for us. If the Spirit draws us to ways of meditation and prayer which do not directly engage with the scriptures, then we would be wise to keep ourselves open to them by means of reading and study. Often the scriptures will become most vivid and alive to us as we prepare to expound them in preaching and teaching. However, we need to guard against the temptation to let our call to preach become the chief motive for investigating the scriptures. We should learn to listen to the needs of our own hearts and search the scriptures for our own healing and revival.

The disciplines of critical biblical study and the spiritual appropriation of Holy Scripture in the heart are commonly treated as incompatible or kept separate. Our community bears a valuable witness in the Church when we demonstrate that intellectual honesty and contemplative openness belong together in our life with Scripture.

If we are truly called by God into this Society we can be sure that the Gospel of John will be an unfailing source of life and light for us. If we become intimately familiar with it by prayer and study, its riches will prove to be limitless. In times of difficulty when we are tempted to turn away we should trust that this gospel will be our rock and mainstay. Entering into it again we shall find ourselves praying the words of Simon Peter to Christ, "Lord, to whom can we go? You have the words of eternal life."

TWENTY-ONE

The Mystery of Prayer

A ceaseless interchange of mutual love unites the Father, Son, and Holy Spirit. Our prayer is not merely communication with God, it is coming to know God by participation in this divine life. In prayer we experience what it is to be made "participants of the divine nature"; we are caught up in the communion of the divine persons as they flow to one another in self-giving love and reciprocal joy. If we hold before us in wonder the mystery of the triune life of God our prayer will realize its full potential. The conception of prayer as homage paid to a distant God will fall away. We shall find ourselves full of awe and gratitude that the life of divine love is open and accessible to us, for God dwells in us. "Those who love me will keep my word, and my Father will love them, and we will come to them and make our home with them." If we begin to accept God's generosity in drawing us into the divine life, and grasp the dignity bestowed on us by the divine indwelling, prayer will spring up in adoration and thanksgiving.

We shall find ourselves adoring the Holy Spirit who is poured out into our hearts and gives us the love with which we can love in return. Our hearts will be filled with thankfulness that the Spirit stirs in the depths of our being and unites all that we are, even what is broken and not yet formed, with the risen Lord. We shall worship Christ himself with adoring love, full of gratitude that he abides in us, and that in him we enjoy the fullness of the Father's acceptance and love. Our contemplation of Christ's undiminished humanity will continually encourage us to offer our selves, our souls and bodies in all their humanity to God through him. Through Christ we shall adore the Father in whom we live and move and have our being, the life-giving mystery of love, who is beyond all words and above all thoughts.

There are many conflicts on the way into the experience of divine love. Sinfulness originates in a deep wound to our humanity which hinders us all from accepting love. As the Spirit exposes it to Christ's healing touch in prayer we shall often have to struggle with our reluctance to be loved so deeply by God. Christ himself will strive with us, as the angel strove with Jacob, to disable our self-reliant pride and make us depend on grace. Our love must be purified and tested by many times of darkness, loss, and waiting. The nearer we draw to God, the more we will sense our vulnerability to the "cosmic powers of this present darkness" that seek to isolate us from God and one another. So there are sufferings to be expected in our prayer but through them we come to the peace Christ promised. "After you have suffered for a little while, the God of all grace, who has called you to his eternal glory in Christ, will himself restore, support, strengthen, and establish you. To him be the power forever and ever. Amen."

TWENTY-TWO

Prayer and Life

God the Holy Spirit longs to inspire in us prayer that includes and embraces the whole of our life. It is a great privilege to be called to the religious life, which offers us every opportunity and encouragement to welcome the Spirit's transforming grace so that prayer may enter more and more into all that we are and all that we do.

Resisting the tendency to restrict prayer to set times, we are to aim at eucharistic living that is responsive at all times and in all places to the divine presence. We should seek the gifts which help us to pray without ceasing. The Spirit offers us the gift of attentiveness by which we discern signs of God's presence and action in creation, in other people, and in the fabric of ordinary existence. We are called to spiritual freedom by which we surrender fretfulness and anxiety in order to be available to God in the present moment. There is the gift of spontaneity, which gives rise to frequent brief prayers throughout the day in which we look to Christ and express our faith, hope, and love. There is the gift of prompt repentance which encourages us to turn to God and ask for forgiveness the instant we become aware of a fall. Through these and other like gifts, prayer comes to permeate our life and transfigure our mundane routines.

The life of prayer calls for the courage to bring into our communion with Christ the fullness of our humanity and the concrete realities of our daily existence, which he redeemed by his incarnation. We are called to offer all our work to God and ask for the graces we need to do it in Christ's name. In our prayer we are to test whether God is confirming our intentions and desires or not. We are able to pray about one another, our relationships and common endeavors. We are to bring him our sufferings and poverty, our passion and sexuality, our fears and resistances, our desires and our dreams, our losses and grief. We must spread before him our cares about the world and its peoples, our friends and families, our enemies and those from whom we are estranged. Our successes and failures, our gifts and shortcomings are equally the stuff of our prayer. We are to offer the night to God, as well as the day, our unconscious selves as well as our conscious minds, acknowledging the secret and unceasing workings of the Spirit in the depths of our hearts.

This deep intention at the heart of our life to find God in all things means learning to trust that divine companionship continues undiminished even when we feel only boredom and frustration. We can learn to stay still in our experience of numbness and resistance, and trust that Christ is just as truly alive in our hearts in these times as in those in which we enjoy the sense of his presence.

The more we discover through prayer how completely the divine presence permeates our life, the greater will be the integrity of our ministry as we teach others to pray. Men and women come to us not merely to learn to pray, but to learn to pray their lives. The prayer which has spread its roots into our whole life bears fruit a hundredfold as we use the resource of our own experience in guiding and initiating others.

TWENTY-THREE

Meditative Prayer

In our meditative prayer each of us seeks intimate communion with God. Quietness and freedom from interruption are needed for us to enter deeply into this prayer. Accordingly, each house of the Society shall have one hour of strict silence set aside each day so that all the brothers can spend this time in meditative prayer completely undisturbed. Occasional necessity may compel a few of us to have their hour of prayer at another time of day, but the community hour is sacrosanct. Although we usually pray alone we are especially close in this hour, bearing one another up. In times of struggle the sense of unity in prayer will be a great support. When we are away on vacation or mission we shall aim at giving half an hour of prayer each day.

"There are varieties of gifts, but the same Spirit." We will not all have the same ways of prayer, but we will be united in seeking to open our hearts to "know the love of Christ that surpasses knowledge, so that [we] may be filled with all the fullness of God." The focus of our meditation may be on the Word of God in Scripture or holy writings. We may use our imaginations to enter into the deep meaning of a scriptural story. Or in slow, reflective reading we may wait for the Spirit to alert us to the words or image which are to be the means of God's particular revelation to us on this day; "the Spirit of truth…will take what is mine and declare it to you." Then meditation opens our minds and hearts, and our response to God's gift and disclosure is kindled by the Spirit within us. God may touch us through icons, images, and symbols, impregnating our hearts with grace and furthering our transformation "from one degree of glory to another." Sometimes God's word is waiting to be heard in our own current experience. The call may be to sift through it in company with Christ to see how he is at work in our lives and where he is leading.

Our prayer may distill our heart's desire in single words or hallowed phrases lovingly repeated, while we lay aside discursive thoughts in order to be unified in Christ. Or we may simply wait on God expectantly until our affections are kindled, and our hearts find a few words to give voice to our worship. When God wills we may be drawn to contemplation. In the radical simplicity of contemplative prayer we surrender ourselves to the mystery beyond words of Christ's abiding in us, and our abiding in him close to the Father's heart.

Meditative prayer is the receptive and responsive prayer of our whole selves. Our bodies are at prayer in the postures and breathing that enable us to be centered. The solitude of the cell gives us the freedom to be spontaneous in expressing prayer through gestures, movements, tears, and singing.

TWENTY-FOUR

The Mystery of Intercession

Father Benson taught us to look always to the glory of the ascended Christ and find the meaning of all we do in union with him. We shall enter into the mystery of intercessory prayer only if we realize our oneness with Christ the great High Priest, who lives forever to make intercession for all the world. Christ makes this prayer to the merciful Father through the prayers of all the faithful who are baptized into his body. His voice does not appeal to God separately from theirs: "They are...so many mouths to Himself; and as they pray...His voice fills their utterance with the authority and claim belonging to Himself." The Father hears the voice of his beloved Son in our prayers and accepts them as Christ's.

It is the Spirit of Christ who stirs our prayer and weaves the movements of our hearts into his great offering. Because the Spirit moves so deeply within us we cannot always be conscious of the full meaning and substance of our prayer. Often our intercessions will feel weak and incoherent. Yet the Spirit is helping us "in our weakness; for we do not know how to pray as we ought, but that very Spirit intercedes with sighs too deep for words. And God, who searches the heart, knows what is the mind of the Spirit, because the Spirit intercedes for the saints according to the will of God."

Through faith we see Christ not only in his majesty in heaven, but in his lowly presence in every creature. He suffers with and in everyone in need. Our intercession does not call down the divine presence to come to the place where we have seen a need, for the Christ who fills all things is already in that place. It is his Spirit who calls us to join him there by offering our love in intercessory prayer and action, to be used by God for healing and transformation.

It is a wonderful thing that God makes us his fellow-workers and uses our love, acting in intercession, to further the reconciliation of all things in Christ. We offer thanks with joy whenever prayer results in the transformation for which we had hoped. However, we must often suffer the pain of seeing no visible result to our prayer. But we should let no frustration wear down the trust that sustains our waiting on God. Every offering of love will bear fruit. "I will do whatever you ask in my name, so that the Father may be glorified in the Son."

According to an ancient monastic saying, "A monk is separated from all and united to all." The pioneers of monasticism believed that the monk was called to the margin of society in order to hear within himself the deepest cries of humanity, and to discover a profound unity with all living beings in their struggle to attain "the freedom of the glory of the children of God." In our intercessory prayer this solidarity will find its deepest expression. We shall also experience through faith our communion with all the saints in glory who pray unceasingly with us and for us.

TWENTY-FIVE

The Practice of Intercession

From the beginning the Church has entrusted to the monastic communities a special responsibility for intercession. Our hearts must always be open to those who ask for our prayers and depend on us to share their burdens. We will rejoice with them when the gift we have sought together from the Lord is given them. And we will stay joined to them in their struggle if God's response seems to deny their request or calls them to wait.

Our prayers for one another, those we serve, the Church and the whole world, the living and the dead, are gathered up in our worship, particularly at the prayers of the people at the Eucharist. We should gladly use the opportunities provided in the liturgy of the Eucharist and in the Daily Office to offer our intercessions aloud as the Spirit moves us.

Once every quarter the community devotes a day to the offering of prayer and fasting. On these days it is our custom to pray together in the presence of the eucharistic elements. Through our fasting and these special times of prayer, we open ourselves so that the Spirit can draw us into the prayer of adoration, and move us to offer intercession for all the people of God.

We shall intercede also in our personal prayers day by day, appealing to God to pour out his saving grace on particular people and situations. In intercession we shall discover the power to love those we find difficult. Father Benson taught that "in praying for others we learn really and truly to love them. As we approach God on their behalf we carry the thought of them into the very being of eternal Love, and as we go into the being of him who is eternal Love, so we learn to love whatever we take with us there." God will also inspire each one of us to make certain causes our special concern. We may also be moved to draw the needs of the world into our contemplative prayer, holding them silently in the radiance of God's mercy within our hearts.

Intercession is not an intermittent activity, restricted to those times in which we are deliberately praying for the world and for people. The entire life of each member of Christ's body is intercessory. Christ takes up our actions and everyday experiences into the eternal offering of his whole self to the Father. If we abide in Christ he will show us that he accepts our labors, our struggles, our afflictions and the ordinary actions of our daily lives as sacrificial, and uses them to bless and uphold the world.

TWENTY-SIX

The Cell and Solitude

The Father of all whom we seek to love is a hidden God. Therefore we take to heart the words of Jesus, "Whenever you pray, go into your room and shut the door and pray to your Father who is in secret; and your Father who sees in secret will reward you." The cell is the place of this secret encounter and reward. From time to time we may choose to pray in chapel, where the icons and sacramental presence of Christ in the tabernacle draw us to contemplation. Or we may pray in a quiet place out of doors. But the cell is the primary place of prayer where we are to stand before God. The cell therefore must be ordered as a space for prayer and treated as sacred. God has promised to be there for us: "Here I will dwell, for I have desired it." As we enter our cells we renew our commitment to meet God there by praying these same words.

We will experience our cell as a place of divine presence and companionship not only in our prayer but in our studying, resting, and sleeping there. There is solace in being alone with God but the privacy of our cells is not meant to shut us off from one another. We gladly welcome one another into our cells for quiet conversations.

Maintaining a balance in our life between solitude and engagement with others is not easy. We are subject to many pressures which deter us from experiencing solitude: the claims of work, the fear of loneliness, and the reluctance to face ourselves as we are in the company of Jesus before God. Without solitude we would forfeit an essential means of inner restoration and encounter with God in the depths of our own souls. Therefore we must find times to be alone. We need to love our cells and take opportunities to stay quietly there in reflection, and in restorative activities such as reading and listening to music. We will need to be disciplined in our use of the radio and recordings so that we use them as means of enrichment rather than of empty distraction. Whenever staying in the cell becomes repugnant to us, or it begins to lose its attraction as a place of solitude, we must remember that we are called to life through death: "Unless a grain of wheat falls into the earth and dies, it remains just a single grain; but if it dies, it bears much fruit." In persevering in our cells we shall discover for ourselves the wisdom of the ancient saying, "The cell will teach you all things."

Our close proximity to one another in our houses means that further solitude may need to be sought elsewhere. We should value opportunities to be alone out of doors and in places where we can be replenished in spirit by ourselves.

Our cells are meant to be congenial and personal places, so we are free to have around us plants, pictures, and other things that beautify them in simple ways. If we clutter the cells with a profusion of objects or make them chaotic and untidy, our rooms will be a hindrance instead of a help to centered, prayerful living. Therefore at least once a year the Superior or Senior Brother shall require each brother to renew the order and simplicity of his cell.

TWENTY-SEVEN

Silence

The gift of silence we seek to cherish is chiefly the silence of adoring love for the mystery of God which words cannot express. In silence we pass through the bounds of language to lose ourselves in wonder. In this silence we learn to revere ourselves also; since Christ dwells in us we too are mysteries that cannot be fathomed, before which we must be silent until the day we come to know as we are known. In silence we honor the mystery present in the hearts of our brothers and sisters, strangers and enemies. Only God knows them as they truly are and in silence we learn to let go of the curiosity, presumption, and condemnation which pretends to penetrate the mystery of their hearts. True silence is an expression of love, unlike the taciturnity that arises from fear and avoidance of relationship.

Silence takes root through our cultivation of solitary prayer in which we are free to take delight in our aloneness with God undisturbed. The Spirit helps us through our struggle with distraction to return to that inmost place of mutual love where God is simply present to us and we to God. If we are faithful here in our movement into silence we will bring the same spirit into our liturgical worship and cherish the silences observed before and during the Eucharist and Offices. Without this constant opening of the heart in silence alone and together, we are unable to feel the touch or hear the word of God. Silence is a constant source of restoration. Yet its healing power does not come cheaply. It depends on our willingness to face all that is within us, light and dark, and to heed all the inner voices that make themselves heard in silence.

Our ministries demand silence for their integrity, in particular our speaking to others and our listening to them in Christ's name. Without silence words become empty. Without silence our hearts would find the burdens, the secrets, and the pain of those we seek to help intolerable and overwhelming. And our ethos of silence is itself a healing gift to those who come to us seeking newness of life.

Each of the disciplines which protect silence in our common life calls for respect. The Greater Silence makes the night and early morning a healing time for recollection. Silent meals and those accompanied by music and reading accustom our guests and us to enjoying fellowship without needing to converse. Appointed days of retreat and quiet invite us to deepen our awareness and prayer. Our cells welcome us into the silence of God's company, and we spurn that welcome if we rely unthinkingly on radio, music, and conversation. We cultivate a thoughtful respect for one another's need to stay focused by avoiding unnecessary interruptions.

Our own strength is not sufficient for weaving silence into the fabric of daily life. For the hours of the day to be permeated by mindfulness of the divine life we must be engaged in constant struggle, depending on God's grace. Powerful forces are bent on separating us from God, our own souls, and one another through the din of noise and the whirl of preoccupation. Technology has intensified our risk of becoming saturated with stimuli. We who are called to maintain a lively interest in our own culture, so that we can bear witness to Christ within it, can never rest from the effort of discernment and resistance or we shall fall captive to scattered-ness and stress.

TWENTY-EIGHT

The Rhythm of Feast and Fast

Jesus chose to work the first of his signs and reveal his glory at the wedding feast at Cana, and he was the chief guest at many meals held to celebrate the new life he was bringing through the gospel. His joy will abound in us when we celebrate by feasting on the holy days that commemorate the great acts of creation and redemption, and the glories of the saints. He will continue to reveal his glory among us on the joyful occasions when we have festal meals to mark professions, clothings, anniversaries, holidays, and special turning points in our life. These feasts are another expression of our eucharistic life, and anticipate the heavenly banquet which the risen Lord is preparing for those who love him. The careful preparations that make our festivities so pleasing are sacred tasks. Our ministry of hospitality finds one of its richest expressions as we welcome guests to join us in these festal liturgies and meals of celebration.

Just as we feast to celebrate the abundance of the risen life, so we also fast because the end is not yet and the bridegroom is still to come. Our feasts will be holy and joyful if we are equally prepared to enter from time to time into Jesus' desert fast. When we fast we should be following him, moved by the Spirit, to offer to God the experience of emptiness and want. This offering is made in faith simply to God's glory, yet from time to time it will open us to the Holy Spirit's work of revelation. In our fasting the Spirit may disclose our need to grieve for sin, ours and the world's. There may be some temptation we will experience more sharply when fasting, and the Spirit can encourage us to struggle with it more directly. Or Christ may want us to sense our connectedness with his countless brothers and sisters who suffer hunger, and embrace their cause in prayer. Above all, the hunger of our fast can open our hearts so that we discover again our hunger and thirst for the living God and have our desire rekindled by the Spirit.

During Lent there will be a common discipline of abstinence with simpler meals and no meat. We will fast by abstaining from food until evening on Ash Wednesday, Good Friday, and the four quarterly days of corporate retreat. We will join brothers in a fast of preparation on the day before they make their vows. On fast days the Superior will give dispensation to those who require some food for reasons of infirmity, medical condition, or unavoidable duties. Those dispensed can participate in other ways through prayer, silence, and recollection. We may fast on our personal retreat days.

Both our feasts and fasts have a part to play in achieving a wise balance in our daily eating and drinking. In our feasting we learn to savor and appreciate what we eat and drink, in thankfulness to the Creator who gives them. Fasting can help us to become more attentive to what our bodies really need so that we can moderate our appetites and be liberated from greed.

TWENTY-NINE

Retreat

Times of retreat are essential elements in the rhythm of our life. They enable us to celebrate the primacy of the love of God above all else. Whenever we enter retreat we seek to be more available to God so that we may enter more fully into the divine life. The community shall have one week of retreat together every year under the direction of a retreat leader. The experience of shared silence and prayer deepens our solidarity in the Spirit and unites us in a common response to the living word. In addition, each professed brother shall have a week of individual retreat every year. The arrangements about the time and place of this retreat will be made in consultation with the Superior. In each quarter of the year there will be a day of corporate retreat, fasting, and intercession. Each brother will have an individual day of retreat every month in which there is no time of community retreat.

Brothers who feel confident of God's call to go forward in the Society will use their retreat before clothing or making their vows to deepen their self-offering to God. If a brother needs further confirmation of the call, the focus of the retreat will be on the discernment of God's will.

Retreat is an opportunity to experience the intimacy we have with God through our union with Christ. Our availability to God will normally be expressed by setting aside three periods for prayer each day, and leaving all distracting tasks. We seek an inner silence for communion with God and therefore refrain from conversation. Exercise and gentle recreative activities in solitude will help us be open to the Spirit.

Retreats will often be times in which we hear Jesus inviting us to be at rest with him: "Come to me, all you that are weary and are carrying heavy burdens, and I will give you rest. Take my yoke upon you, and learn from me; for I am gentle and humble in heart, and you will find rest for your souls." But we must expect retreats to expose us to spiritual trial. We may be tempted to tire ourselves or waste the time in busy work and preparation. We may find ourselves staying on the surface to avoid an authentic meeting with the living God. And the emptiness of retreat time may compel us to face painful signs of our need for healing which it was easier to overlook during our usual routines. So our retreat times will be opportunities to strive against everything that would discourage us from radical dependence on the love of God.

Those of us who guide the retreats of others should be creative in our own use of retreat and guard against mere routine. Our own experience must be real and vital if we are to draw on it when we guide those who are seeking God.

THIRTY

Guidance and Reconciliation

In our own prayer Christ will come to us as a servant seeking to wash our feet, but he also seeks to attend to our needs through the ministry of others and the Church's sacraments of nurture, forgiveness, and healing. We fall and fall again so we should be glad of the opportunities that the sacramental rite of Reconciliation provides to encounter Christ again in the places of our brokenness and poverty, and allow him to bind up our wounds and set us on our feet. If we ever feel reluctant to use this means of grace we must remember how Peter was tempted to refuse the touch of Christ, and how the Lord had to warn him of its necessity. The Superior ensures that each brother has regular access to a confessor outside the community. We are to make our confessions at least every quarter.

We cannot keep pace with the risen Christ who goes before us if we are encumbered by guilt. If we stay estranged in our hearts we jeopardize the communion we have with our brothers and our fellow members of the Body of Christ. Regular sacramental confession enables us to shed the burdens of remembered sin, and to move forward encouraged by the Spirit. We enter the fellowship of the community again with fresh gratitude for the reality of forgiveness. Father Benson has taught us to live as penitents, "to rise thus to live in the full light of the presence of Jesus, to rise to have nothing hidden, to live in openness of heart to Him, and in an openness of heart to one another also, which the world does not know of, to tear away the veil which hides our hearts, to have our inmost life standing out in the presence of God."

Each brother in vows, after consulting with the Superior, will find a spiritual director with whom to meet regularly. Christ is not only the Lamb of God who takes away the sin of the world, he is "the way, and the truth, and the life." In spiritual direction we make progress on the way which is Christ, learning how we go astray and discovering the paths of prayer and mercy. Our spiritual directors help us enter into the truth which is Christ, uncovering our illusions and guiding us to explore the freedom for which Christ has set us free. They challenge us to seek liberation from all that is narrow and superficial so that we can find the abundance of life which is Christ. Anyone who tries self-sufficiency in the spiritual life soon falls prey to illusion. From the earliest days God has given members of our Society the calling and gifts for the ministry of spiritual direction. It is especially important for those of us who are called to be spiritual directors to receive direction ourselves.

Christ will also make himself known as the good shepherd through the teaching and counsel of our retreat leaders. In times of retreat we should open our hearts, expecting to hear his voice speaking through the one we have invited to guide us.

THIRTY-ONE

Mission and Service

Christ sends us with the same passionate trust and love with which the Father sent him into the world. Our mission is to bring men, women, and children into closer union with God in Christ, by the power of the Spirit that he breathes into us. Christ is already present in the life of everyone as the light of the world. It is our joy to serve all those to whom we are sent by helping them to embrace that presence in faith. Our mission is being fulfilled as our prayer, worship, and daily life in community draw people into life in Christ. It is also expressed through ministries which demonstrate the wide range of the Spirit's gifts. These ministries spring from our baptismal vocation; only a few of them are the specific responsibility of the ordained. The Society's identity is not defined by any particular ministries since the Spirit is free to change them. Nevertheless, our tradition, experience, and discernment of the signs of our own times encourage us to be alert for Christ's invitation to serve in the following ways.

We are ready to respond to the needs of those who desire to learn how to pray, to understand the things of the Spirit, and to press forward on the way of conversion. Some brothers therefore make themselves available, as the Spirit enables them, for ministries of spiritual formation, initiation, and guidance with individuals and with groups, both in the Church and where there are seekers outside. We will be alert to the claims of those who seek solid nourishment for the heart and mind, and be open to God's call to preach, to teach, and to provide written resources through books and publications.

God may prolong our tradition of service to those who are exercising, or being prepared for, ordained ministry in the Church by calling us to support them with our hospitality, to act as guides and confessors, and to offer such training as we may be qualified to give. Equally, we are ready to support and equip lay men and women for their ministries.

God may call us to further the work of healing and reconciliation by reaching out to the sick, offering the sacraments of healing and forgiveness, befriending the alienated and perplexed, serving those in prison, and seeking the company of the marginalized.

We are to be prepared for God to call us to be active witnesses for peace and social justice, bearing witness to Christ's presence on the side of people who are deprived and oppressed. We expect our calling to continue to bring special resources to bear on the needs and claims of children and their families in places where they are impoverished and at risk.

God may call a few of us to special ventures in mission in other places and countries, or to hold office in the Church. In rare cases where a brother would be separated from community life for long periods we would look for clear signs that this was indeed a call coming from God. In our understanding and discernment of ministry we must be careful to recognize how broad is the range of talents that God uses in ministry, being prepared for ministries which draw on artistic gifts and engage our concerns for the environment and the renewal of society.

THIRTY-TWO

The Spirit of Mission and Service

A ll our ministries are expressions of our community life; they are carried out in the name of the whole Society, supported by its prayers and the labors of those who carry on the other regular work of our daily life. All of us share in the graces that flow from them. While strictly respecting the confidentiality which covers many aspects of our work, we should share the rest of our experiences in ministry with one another so that we can appreciate them and give praise to God together. Wherever possible we shall go out on mission in twos and threes rather than singly so that we can express our companionship in ministry.

Certain brothers bear their part in our mission chiefly by sustaining the life of the community with their work, witness, and prayer at home. It is important to express our awareness of their vital role within the body. This sense of our interdependence and equality will be especially important for the infirm and elderly.

Christ has promised that if we abide in him and consent to his skillful pruning, we shall bear fruit that abides. If the results of our labors are to last we need to root our endeavors in Christ and draw on our intimacy with him. This involves prayer for ourselves and for those whose lives we have the opportunity to touch. Knowing that grace is powerful in weakness, we hand over to Christ any anxiety about our own adequacy. We are to trust our own experience of God and draw directly from it so that our witness can be authentic. We also need to let go of any grasping for immediate results; much of what the grace of God achieves through us will be entirely hidden from our eyes. We also expect to experience failures. Some of these contain lessons which can help us become more skillful in the future. Other failures are means by which we enter further into the mystery of discipleship; we are not greater than the master, and many went on their way without accepting his words or deeds.

If we give freely of ourselves, we should expect abundant gifts in return, according to Christ's promise. We should enter into our ministries expecting to receive as much or more than we can give. Christ will make himself known to us in wonderful ways in those we serve, especially in those who suffer and are poor in spirit. Ministry itself will draw out from us gifts, insights, and strengths which we never knew we had. We will be continually taught, humbled, surprised, and stretched. Ministry is itself a vital means of our conversion by Christ and its disciplines are central to our asceticism. We must also expect power to go out of us in ministry and to experience fatigue which may sometimes be severe. Seasons of rest and relief are important for individual brothers and the whole community.

THIRTY-THREE

Ministry in Practice

Discerning which opportunities for ministry we should respond to brings into play the wisdom of the whole community, the responsibility of particular brothers, and the skillful supervision of the Superior. In deciding which ventures to pursue or invitations to accept we take into account the resources of the community, the availability of particular brothers and their needs, and the mission priorities of the Society, as well as the needs of those whose claims upon us are under consideration. We must remember that we are called to exercise demanding ministries within the community for one another and among our employees and those who work alongside us. The prudence which informs this practice of discernment is not meant to hold us back from responding generously and spontaneously to unforeseen and urgent claims that the Spirit makes upon us.

The coordination of our tasks, responsibilities, and ministries means that we must often turn down requests and opportunities. Without faithfulness to our limitations we can jeopardize our community life and its balance. It will often be painful when we are unable to respond to needs which touch our hearts. It is important to share this frustration in prayer. Christ can help us to accept our limitations as expressions of our poverty, and the constraints he imposes as ways in which he is shaping and molding our lives. In a community such as ours it is unrealistic to expect that the balance between meeting our own needs and those of others can be kept always in perfect equilibrium. Instead we must be resilient enough to embrace the emergencies and stresses which belong to apostolic life.

Our reliance on the spontaneity of the Holy Spirit in our ministry does not replace the need for training, preparation, and supervision. We may only engage in ministries for which we have received training and whose disciplines we have embraced. It is especially important in those ministries which involve confidential work with individuals that we observe those boundaries and guidelines which are binding on ministers of the Church. A brother must never be left feeling isolated in his ministry. The leaders of the community must make sure that resources of consultation and supervision are available to him.

We make it known to groups and individuals who call upon our ministries that the Society needs donations to support our work. Normally we help them in the exercise of their stewardship by suggesting amounts in proportion to our outlay of time and effort. God's generosity in supplying all our needs gives us the freedom to make our ministries available to certain groups and individuals who lack the resources to make these normal donations.

THIRTY-FOUR

Hospitality

The source of hospitality is the heart of God who yearns to unite every creature within one embrace. Only in the fullness of time will God gather all things in Christ, yet God's boundless welcome is something we already enjoy here and now in the Eucharist. Our life together as a community gives us a foretaste of the communion of saints. So we have the power to be a sacrament of God's hospitality, a house of God, offering his nurture and protection to all who come under our roof.

It is not enough merely to offer accommodation to visitors. Our faith must recognize the one who comes to us in the person of the guest, the stranger, and the pilgrim. It is the Lord, who has identified himself with each of his sisters and brothers. If we are to give them bread and not stones, and truly meet Christ in them face to face, we must realize the gifts the Holy Spirit has given us for the ministry of hospitality, and remember how deeply people are yearning for the things of God. We have silence for our guests, which protects the mystery of their hearts and brings healing. We have our ongoing stream of worship, which they can enter. We have the fellowship of our altar and our table. We offer security, where guests are safe from intrusion and free to pray. Our houses have simple beauty. We offer courtesy, acceptance, and intercession. And the Spirit has given us gifts of guidance, teaching, and encouragement by which we can help retreatants grow in Christ.

We must also remain true to the limits of our hospitality. The claims of our life together and our other ministries mean we cannot take in everyone who wants to come or meet a guest's every need. We cannot offer the closeness that some are seeking and can seldom be available as pastoral counselors. Normally our guests can stay only for short periods. If we let our life as a brotherhood be overwhelmed by the claims of guests we could endanger the resources by which we can serve them. We can be confident of the rightness of boundaries which contain and foster our own life together. Every house shall have a private area to which guests are not normally invited and there shall be interludes during the year when guests are not received. The brothers who are given primary responsibility for our ministry of hospitality know its cost more than any and they need our support. Not every guest will be easy to welcome. If we experience difficulties in our relationship with any guests we should pray specially to find Christ in them and consult one another about the most appropriate resolution.

Just as we enrich our guests' lives, so they enrich ours. We welcome men and women of every race and culture, rejoicing in the breadth and diversity of human experience that they bring to us. Their lives enlarge our vision of God's world. The stories of their sufferings and achievements and their experience of God stir and challenge us. If we are attentive, each guest will be a word and gift of God to us.

THIRTY-FIVE

Employees

Among our many partners in ministry the men and women who earn their living by working for the Society have a special place. We could not fulfill the mission to which God calls us without the contribution of their many skills which complement our own. Our concern and gratitude for them should find frequent expression in our prayers.

Our belief in the dignity of work and the honor due to all forms of labor and creativity should be revealed by the respect we show to each of our employees. The way we exercise authority as employers must reveal our belief in the equality of all as persons and citizens. We know that for many of our employees the work they undertake for us is the chief expression of their ministry within the Body of Christ. Their dedication often leads them to give more than duty requires. It is important that we regularly show our appreciation and gratitude in a variety of ways.

To help in maintaining the highest standards of integrity, fairness, and clarity we shall use a manual of guidelines setting out all the procedures to be observed in our professional relationships with our employees. It is an important feature of community discipline to be faithful to these rules. The brother responsible for human resources guides those who supervise individual employees. Our commitment to the well-being of our employees includes a concern for their professional development and continuing education as well as fair compensation and time off.

The nature of our community life and ministries leads us to require our employees to be especially respectful of our privacy, and to maintain confidentiality about ourselves and our guests. We, for our part, must demonstrate our commitment to this ethos of confidentiality and refrain from any kind of inappropriate intrusion into the personal lives of our employees.

THIRTY-SIX

New Members

New members bring with them the promise of new life for our brotherhood. They contribute new gifts for our common good and our mission, both personal talents and gifts of the Holy Spirit. This promise of newness of life and hope for the future should be a source of joy. We shall often pray to the Father for the gift of new members, trusting that our prayer will be answered: "Very truly, I tell you, if you ask anything of the Father in my name, he will give it to you."

It is an important responsibility for the Novice Guardian and Superior to lead the community in a collective process of discernment to discover whether an applicant is genuinely drawn to our way of life and has certain basic qualities which are necessary. Through observation, prayer, and conversation we seek to find that the candidate has a love for the gospel, a desire for prayer, an attraction to ministry, and signs of personal adaptability. We also draw on the results of professional testing to provide evidence that his mental and physical health are adequate for the demands of our life.

Postulancy is a preliminary test of a man's calling. Normally it lasts for six months but the Superior may lengthen or shorten the time as he sees fit. The postulant takes part in the life and duties of the novices so that we can discover whether he has the resilience and maturity to set out on the path of formation. The postulancy culminates in a directed retreat. If the postulant then shows a strong desire to go forward, the Superior will decide whether to admit him to the novitiate, first consulting the Novice Guardian.

Integration into a brotherhood like ours is a slow process. Brothers are to be welcoming and supportive to those who are with us for a trial period. At first the bonds we establish with new members will be light, allowing them to feel unconstrained in their freedom to leave. Deeper mutual commitment comes later. It is important that the professed brothers express their considered reactions to the new member's early days of adjustment when they meet to conduct evaluations.

Our sober recognition that only a few of those who come to test their vocation will go forward to life profession ought not to discourage us as we initiate new men into our way of life. We trust that God always uses a man's time in our Society for good. Every call is entirely in God's hands.

THIRTY-SEVEN

The Novitiate

The novitiate is a time of progressive initiation into the life of the community. Novices are putting their vocation to the test of experience. At first they participate in our active ministries only in limited ways, so that they can devote themselves with a single mind to conversion of life. Their training is in the hands of the Novice Guardian; the Superior will help him and appoint at least two other experienced brothers to assist with the work of formation and discernment.

We are to help the novices to let go of their previous life and work, and to come to a changed understanding of their relationship with family and friends that makes room for their new and primary loyalty to the Society. We expect them to grow into our full life of worship and prayer and offer them training in spiritual disciplines. Recognizing that our novices will not have had the same exposure to the resources of Christian knowledge and wisdom, we will guide them in corporate and individual study that will help each brother explore the scriptures, Christian doctrine, history, and spirituality. We help them to grasp the meaning of this Rule and to explore our particular tradition and the teaching of our founders. The novices begin to make the Gospel of John their own, and to understand the role of the monastic way in the life and mission of the Church, past and present. We give our novices work in which they have opportunity to practice obedience and cooperation, learn humility, and discover within themselves a readiness to act with generosity.

Growing into our life under this Rule is not a matter of mere adaptation but of inner change and conversion of life. We expect emotional and spiritual trials to be part of the experience of the novitiate; many stages of genuine transformation are marked by experiences of confusion and loss. The brothers who have a special responsibility for the work of formation help the novices to face these trials with courage and to gain insight into their meaning.

The other professed brothers participate in the formation of novices in many ways. Novices learn the meaning of our vocation from our daily witness to the mercy of God and the graces of the vowed life. Our encouragement enables them to endure the stresses of adjustment and change. Their readiness for commitment is fostered by the faithfulness of our prayerful friendship. And we contribute our insights into their development by means of the regular evaluation sessions.

Our hope is that the novitiate will lead to the discovery of an inner freedom to choose this life gladly, or to take up again the challenge of Christian life outside, if this seems God's will. The novitiate normally lasts two years. Towards the end of the second year the Superior shall consult with those who train the novices, and decide whether to propose to the Chapter the election of the novice to profession in initial vows. The novitiate may be extended, but not beyond a third year. Every novice prepares for profession in a retreat of two weeks.

THIRTY-EIGHT

Initial Profession

The whole community rejoices when a new brother is ready to make the vows of poverty, celibacy, and obedience. His aim should be towards life commitment, even though at first he is allowed to bind himself by the vows for a period of three years only. This initial period gives time for the community and the brother to make certain that God is calling him to the life of our Society.

Through his discussions with the brother at the end of the period of commitment in initial vows the Superior may conclude that it is wise to extend it for a further year. Three such extensions are permitted.

The years of initial profession are dedicated to further formation in the religious life. This is a time to begin discerning the gifts a brother may have for ministry, and providing opportunities for developing these gifts through training and practice. His studies should not be directed to these ministries alone, but should aim at a further consolidation of his knowledge of Scripture and the classics of Christian theology and wisdom. During these years the brother develops a firmer grasp of his identity as a religious and seeks to intensify his self-offering to God in daily life and work.

The newly professed brother takes his place in Chapter and begins to take a full part in the community's decision-making. He becomes eligible for new responsibilities and tasks.

An important goal of these initial years in vows is the development of personal responsibility for one's own growth in the religious life and a strong sense of accountability. To promote this development, each brother in initial vows will meet regularly to discuss his own progress with an experienced brother, or group of brothers, appointed by the Superior to provide him with support and advice. In addition, every nine months or so, the Superior and one or two of these appointed brothers will gather for a day of assessment with the brother in initial vows. In this assessment he gives a full account of his experience of life under this Rule, discusses goals to aim for in the coming months, and receives counsel.

We pray that when the moment of decision comes, our brother will find that Christ has given him the freedom and courage to choose life-long commitment. The foundation of this courage is a profound gratitude for salvation. "How shall I repay the Lord for all the good things he has done for me? I will lift up the cup of salvation and call upon the Name of the Lord. I will fulfill my vows to the Lord in the presence of all his people." Before accepting his application to be admitted to life profession, the Superior must consult with each member of Chapter to gather evidence that we share the conviction that God is calling him. The final decision rests with the Superior. The brother prepares for life profession in a retreat of at least two weeks.

THIRTY-NINE

Life Profession

Jesus' offering of his life on the cross was the supreme expression of his love for the Father, made in perfect freedom through the Spirit. "No one takes it from me, but I lay it down of my own accord." This free self-offering is expressed anew in our lives when, abiding in Christ, we find in him the power to surrender ourselves entirely to God by taking the vows of poverty, celibacy, and obedience for life. When a brother vows to abide in our community until death, the whole brotherhood rejoices in the gift of freedom which enables him to make this commitment after years of testing.

Father Benson has taught us that the call of God in the religious life is continuous, abiding, and progressive. Continuous, because in the communion we enjoy with God in prayer and worship day by day the voice of the Spirit never ceases to call us into deeper union. Abiding, because the wisdom of God, communicated to us in our prayer and life, is absorbed into our hearts never to perish. Progressive, because God's voice will come to us in the future ever new, calling us to fresh opportunities, and bringing gifts beyond what we know now. As profession brings to an end the period of probation, so it inaugurates a lifetime of developing response. As a community we are responsible for making sure that each brother has the encouragement to grow and change in response to the life-giving Spirit through whom we are born again. Periodically the Superior will invite each brother in life vows to take part in a day of assessment with him. This provides an opportunity for the brother to reflect deeply on the call of God and his response to it. The Superior will invite one or two other brothers to take part in the discussions.

The life profession of a brother inspires us with awe as well as joy; we wonder at the risk of such a decisive choice. For a time may come when his steadfastness could be tried to the limits of endurance. He may then long to take back his promise, and leave us. Setbacks and disappointments will shake his constancy. He may be tempted to use changes that have taken place in the Society, in the Church, or in himself as pretexts for canceling his commitment. Only by depending on God for the grace of perseverance, fixing ourselves by faith in God's unwavering commitment to us, can we risk taking vows which bind us forever. A life profession will be a special opportunity to renew our confidence that grace will not fail us. "If what you heard from the beginning abides in you, then you will abide in the Son and in the Father."

The grace to surrender our lives to God through our vows has been given to us in Baptism whereby we die with Christ and are raised with him. It is the same grace that gives strength to the martyrs to submit gladly to death as witnesses of the resurrection. From the beginning monks and nuns have been encouraged to understand their own commitment in the light of the freedom and trust which enables martyrs to give up their lives to the glory of God. The witness of the martyrs should never be far from our minds as we go forward in the vowed life day by day.

FORTY

Separation from the Society

Our pilgrimage as religious will be marked by separations, when members leave the community. These partings on the way will test the quality of our brotherly love and our dependence on God alone.

Separations may give rise to many different responses. When it has become clear that a novice or brother in initial vows does not have a vocation to our life we may feel gladness that he is ready to move on to explore God's call to another way; even so, if we have grown to love one another, the separation will wound us. But when a brother leaves because he has ceased to rise up to the demands of God's call, our grief will be more severe. Only truth sets us free, and the Spirit of truth will help all of us to express and face the conflicting emotions we may feel. While some brothers are experiencing anger and disappointment, others may be more conscious of relief. There may be times when we recognize that the departure of a member clears away an obstacle to the onward movement of the community. We can help one another accept the validity of our different feelings and support one another as we work through them.

The same Spirit who frees us through the truth is the Spirit of love, who will give us in due course the generosity to let our brother go with respect and hope, commending him to the love of God. In the Spirit we will be able to trust that God had a holy purpose in calling him to be a member of our brotherhood for a time. As part of our continuous self-examination as a community, we will go on to consider together what there may be for us to learn from his leaving.

It may happen that a brother in life vows comes to feel he is unable to persevere, and expresses a desire to leave the Society. The gravity of this crisis means that the community and he must embark on a process of discernment of a year's duration to discover whether his vocation is dead, or whether the breakdown can be healed. Only after this may the Chapter release him from his membership of the Society. His vows remain binding until he is dispensed from them by the Visitor.

Whenever a man leaves, there is an opportunity for us to recognize the mystery of our vocation and to reaffirm our total dependence on God for the grace of perseverance. Jesus gave a special calling to the beloved disciple to remain until his coming. We can be steadfast only if we grow in reliance day by day on the glory of Christ's faithful abiding in us.

FORTY-ONE

The Maturing of Our Minds in Christ

Our pursuit of knowledge is an expression of love for God's world and the riches of revelation. As we bring our gifts of imagination and intellect to maturity we are able to glorify God more and more. Since our gifts and ministries vary we need to encourage one another to value not only reading and study but many other ways of learning, every method that helps us become more responsive in heart and mind to the whole creation. As our faith matures we come to recognize Christ's hidden presence everywhere: "All things have been created through him and for him. He himself is before all things, and in him all things hold together."

We cannot fulfill our mission without a lifelong engagement with the riches of Scripture and the Christian tradition. We need therefore to encourage and train one another to explore this great tradition firsthand. It is important to absorb classics of Christian spirituality and theology, and valuable for each of us to develop a personal interest in certain schools, periods, or figures to which we might be specially drawn. We need knowledge of other faiths, and a sound grasp of religious history to which good biographies have given richness and color.

The Spirit calls us to be alert and open to our own time. Some of us will be drawn to contemporary explorations of theology and spirituality and engage in studies that throw light on the changes now taking place in the world. Our aim is to maintain a lively, critical interest in the cultures in which we are situated, and seek to expand our perspectives globally so that we can empathize with other societies and religious traditions.

All our ministries, whether of preaching, teaching, or personal encounter in the Spirit, call for a penetrating understanding of the mysteries of the heart and human relationships. For this we need many resources. Psychology and the human sciences are sources of insight, and some of us will find in literature, philosophy, drama, film, music, dance, and the visual arts springs of vital truth if we approach them keenly in the Spirit.

We commit ourselves to maintaining ample libraries in each house as well as devoting funds for further education and the enrichment of the imagination. The community is to hold regular events of corporate education so that our learning can be a shared experience. Individual commitment to learning in a disciplined way is equally essential. Study does not have the same attraction for all of us, and even those who enjoy it find that the pressure of other responsibilities distracts them. Unless we grasp the truth that it is both a labor of love and a spiritual discipline, we are likely to neglect study. We should therefore support one another in regularly setting aside time for reading, and encourage one another to take advantage of opportunities for training, enrichment, and further education. Our sense of common endeavor will be stimulated when we discuss with one another what we are learning and take a mutual interest in our discoveries. Our goal is to arrive at the maturity which enables us to plan our study so that it can be focused, regular, and supported. We shall not often be able to reserve time for study every day, but each week should include it.

FORTY-TWO

The Graces of Friendship

No one has greater love than this, to lay down one's life for one's friends. You are my friends if you do what I command you. I do not call you servants any longer, because the servant does not know what the master is doing; but I have called you friends, because I have made known to you everything that I have heard from my Father."

For us no honor exists that could be greater than Jesus calling us his friends. The more we enter into the fullness of our friendship with him, the more he will move us to be friends for one another, and to cherish friendship itself as a means of grace. The forging of bonds between us that would make us ready to lay down our lives for one another is a powerful witness to the reality of our risen life in Christ. In an alienating world, where so many are frustrated and wounded in their quest for intimacy, we can bear life-giving testimony to the graces of friendship as men who know by experience its demands, its limitations, and its rewards.

Among ourselves we must devote time, energy, and prayer to the fostering of friendship. There are many different degrees of intensity in celibate friendship, and stages of growth. Our common concerns are to lay aside perfectionism, to respect the variety of bonds which we will establish between us, and to ensure that none is left friendless. "Where the Spirit of the Lord is, there is freedom";

we shall seek to let go of possessiveness and extend this freedom to one another. We want to have the freedom continually to release our brother for relationship with others, just as in those dances in which the movements constantly weave fresh links between the dancers.

We also have opportunities to make friends outside the community. Friends of different ages, cultures, and walks of life will enrich our humanity. We value the gift of friendship with women, as Jesus did; without it we run the risk of spiritual and personal impoverishment. But there are costly constraints to be accepted on both sides in the friendships between religious and others, and discretion needs to be fostered with those outside. In particular it is vital that we protect the confidentiality of one another's personal lives and the privacy of the Society's inner life.

The Spirit uses the demands of friendship to further our conversion; struggles are inevitable as well as rewards. Our sexuality, our dread of rejection and disappointment, our need for forgiveness and reconciliation, our difficulties in achieving emotional honesty are all brought into play. Fear can hold us back. In these struggles we have the constant companionship of Christ to give us courage and joy.

FORTY-THREE

Mutual Support and Encouragement

Each day brings fresh opportunities to fulfill the commandment of Christ "that you love one another as I have loved you." We need one another's support at times of special stress, disappointment, and weakness, but we also need it as the daily bread of our life together. Encouragement is expressed not only through serious concern for one another but also through the free play of our God-given sense of humor.

Honest and direct communication help us strengthen one another. We create the setting for mutual disclosure about how we are experiencing our life in regular meetings from which we exclude the discussion of business. In these, and our other sessions for planning and discussion, we are called to engage one another openly. A brother can frustrate that openness if he shuts himself off or does too much talking. On the other hand, insensitivity in the gathering can inhibit a brother from sharing from the heart. We shall need to invite the Spirit constantly to build up our trust and show us how to speak the truth in love.

We can lift one another up through celebration and the practice of courtesy. We value the opportunities which birthdays and anniversaries present for celebrating a brother's life. And we seek to sustain a climate of courtesy in which each of us receives assurance day by day that he is appreciated. We need to be generous in expressing delight in one another's achievements.

We express our regard for one another not only in words, but in gestures which give our bodies a part to play in the interchange of affection, as is natural for men who believe wholeheartedly in the incarnation. We are free to cheer one another with open arms of welcome and to show our care and sensitivity through touch.

Like Jesus, we will be especially attentive to those who could easily become isolated or overlooked. Newcomers to our life, the older brothers, and those who are in pain from illness, sorrow, or spiritual trial have particular claims on our hearts. The Superior of the community bears burdens for us all which become intolerable if brothers neglect to express their care for him regularly and explicitly, or fail to cherish him when he is under pressure.

Above all, we are to open our hearts to any brother with whom we are in conflict. Breaches of trust, injuries, even enmity are bound to happen since communities of love are special targets of evil forces. These forces will tempt us to defer reconciliation, or even to pretend that the fabric of our common life has not been torn. But the Spirit of the crucified and risen Christ spurs us to seek out the one from whom we feel estranged in order to establish communion with him again through a mutual change of heart.

FORTY-FOUR

Maintaining Our Health and Creativity

Jesus came as our healer that we "may have life, and have it abundantly." We show our lack of faith in him if we diminish that abundance through neglect, or the fear Jesus portrayed in the parable of the man who buried the talent his master had committed to him.

Health of mind, body, and spirit is a priceless gift of the Creator which we are to cherish in wonder and thankfulness: "I will thank you because I am marvelously made; your works are wonderful, and I know it well." So that we can better glorify God in our bodies each of us shall take responsibility for maintaining his health through regular exercise, hygiene, and prompt recourse to medical attention as soon as he becomes aware of any significant symptom. Hypochondria and obsessive self-concern, on the other hand, are distortions of this duty and it is our responsibility to call one another to maturity.

If a brother shows signs of disorder in his relation to food, alcohol, or any other substance, this becomes the concern of the whole community. The Superior has the responsibility of helping him to set his feet on the path of sobriety, moderation, and health.

Likewise the compulsion to overwork and other forms of obsessive behavior are signs that freedom is lacking and healing needed.

Each of us has been given the divine spark of creativity and imagination, and as we grow in our conversion to Christ, so should our gratitude and reverence for these gifts. Fear and inertia quench the spirit. Faith in the Giver of all good gifts will lead us to use the opportunities our life provides for developing our creativity and using our imagination. The community shall provide time and resources for hobbies and skillful pursuits so that every brother may find outlets for creativity beyond what his regular work offers. We shall seek to maintain a climate where music and other arts are valued and where the beauty of creation is loved and enjoyed. We shall endeavor to order our stewardship so that vacations can provide not only the opportunity of visiting our families and friends but also of exposure to the beauties of nature, the stimulus of other cultures, and enrichment by the arts. Our creativity will thrive on mutual encouragement.

If our endeavor to develop our creativity were in response to a secular ideal of self-realization it would come to nothing. Our stretching towards fullness of life is an act of faith in Christ who is the living Word through whom all things have their being. He is the true light shining through all creation. It is not in religious activity and thought alone that we see his glory, but in all the world. We are called to realize his life-giving presence within our own selves and bodies and to share in his ongoing creation.

FORTY-FIVE

Rest and Recreation

The hallowing of rest and the keeping of sabbath is an essential element in our covenant with God. The one who can find no happiness except in ceaseless work is afraid to be still and know that the Lord alone is God. If we find ourselves filling leisure time with tasks we can be sure that we have begun to imagine that our worth consists in what we accomplish. When we regularly cease from our labor and enjoy rest as a holy gift we can grow in trust that our worth in God's sight lies simply in our very being, clothed with Christ.

In the culture in which we live the pressures to be busy all the time are intense, and it is a true ascetic endeavor to resist them in obedience to God. The Church itself is in constant danger of adapting to a culture of hyperactivity and stress. We have a particular call to resist this conformity and to bear witness before the world to the graciousness and wisdom of the sabbath. Our faithfulness will show itself in our attention to the needs of the body and spirit for sleep and rest. Our life is demanding and we must recognize how much power goes out of us in our ministry. By taking rest we show that we accept our creaturely need for replenishment and restoration, as Jesus did.

Our ministries of hospitality, preaching, liturgy, and retreat direction mean that Sunday usually makes many demands on our energies. Although the Lord's day itself cannot be our actual day of rest, we should seek through our prayer on Sunday to lift up our hearts in the joy of the resurrection. Because our rest comes on another day of the week it is all the more important to recall the sacredness of sabbath time.

The ways each of us will enjoy our sabbath day will be many and varied, but each of us will need to distinguish between leisure that is genuinely recreative and the drifting which comes from sloth. Our day of rest gives us the opportunity to refresh and deepen our friendships. It enables us to play and exercise and enjoy the use of our senses. It opens a space for music, art, entertainment, and particular pursuits and hobbies. The fruits of our leisure time will prove whether we have hallowed or profaned our sabbath. If we have kept it holy we will resume our daily life reinvigorated and restored to ourselves. If we have wasted our leisure, we may find our day off leaving us with a sense of dullness and a residue of fatigue. We can help one another use our leisure time well by taking care not to give one another needless tasks on our day of rest.

Holy rest has its place in the rhythm of each day as well as the week. Those who reserve a time each day for some leisure which brings composure and refreshment set a good example for all the brothers to follow. The sabbath commandment is also a guide for our well-being in the longer view. We shall endeavor to provide opportunities for special times of renewal from time to time, especially when a brother has had some years of hard work in a particular ministry.

In each house of the Society the brothers shall gather regularly to enjoy conversation in a relaxed atmosphere. All should partici-pate so that the common life may be strengthened.

FORTY-SIX

The Challenges
of Sickness

We are co-creators with the Holy Spirit who enables us to consecrate every aspect of life as an offering to God's glory. Even sickness can be transfigured, and become the means by which we experience personally the reality of the Lord's assurance, "My grace is sufficient for you, for my power is made perfect in weakness." A brother's illness affects the whole community and God will provide gifts of grace for us all.

The fragility of human life makes sickness inevitable. When it befalls us we are to seek restoration and play our full part in the process of healing. This means radical dependence on Christ through our own prayer, the prayer of the community and our friends, and his ministry of healing mediated through the sacramental rite of the Laying on of Hands and Anointing. It involves our ready acceptance of medical means of healing. The whole community joins the brother in his rejoicing when he is restored to health.

Sickness may compel us to be dependent on the care of others. This may conflict with our pride and challenge our notion of self-sufficiency. We are called to let go and accept the service of others gracefully. It is an important expression of our vow of obedience to be open and cooperative with those who are looking after us in sickness. Those who care for the sick should cherish this opportunity of service and realize that their caring may be the chief means by which the sufferer experiences the companionship and love of Christ.

Physical and mental illness may bring such suffering that our faith in God is put to the test. Our prayer for healing may not be answered in the way we desire. We may have to come to terms with disability or incurable sickness. Pain and fear may make us feel abandoned by God. The springs of prayer may seem to dry up. All of us should live day by day in growing dependence on Christ crucified so that we are prepared for such times of trial. Our life is hidden with Christ in God. God suffers with us. In times of pain, when we are aware only of darkness, we will need sheer faith to assure us that we are still inseparably united to the God of love.

A brother may be so sick that he cannot play an active part in the liturgy and our ministries. But we should trust that the offering of sickness and weakness contributes powerfully to our total life in Christ. Those who suffer are "completing what is lacking in Christ's afflictions for the sake of his body, that is, the church." And those of us who have been strengthened by God in sickness are able to use their experience to "console those who are in any affliction with the consolation with which we ourselves are consoled by God."

The Gifts and Challenges of Old Age

Tradition records that the beloved disciple lived to a great age. We who belong to a community named after him are called to be appreciative of the gifts that come to maturity in old age, and also sensitive to the needs and struggles that accompany it.

We pray that seeds planted in many years of faithful life will bear fruit in old age. Our older brothers will then be able to contribute their experience of what is essential in our life with God, a sense of perspective, wisdom, their appreciation for the community, and joy in the younger members. The elders of the community are to be honored as the bearers of our corporate memory who link us with our past. Some of us will even reach our prime in old age, discovering new gifts and continuing active in ministry informed by long experience.

We grieve to see the old so commonly neglected and discounted in the world around us. The way we honor and cherish one another in advancing years can be a powerful witness against this sinful failure. Our valuing of elderly brothers becomes particularly important when the limitations of old age prevent them from participating very fully in our active ministries. We need to ensure that the spirituality of the community, expressed in our teaching, conversation, and actions, affirms the intrinsic worth of every member and emphasizes the contributions that the elders make through their prayer and perseverance. Unless there is this climate of support, an older brother may give way to discouragement, or have difficulty in accepting a role in the community with fewer responsibilities and restricted opportunities.

Our closing years of earthly life may bring new challenges in the spiritual combat. It is humbling to grow more dependent on the care of others. It is hard to cooperate with the Spirit and overcome our natural tendency to deny our decreasing strength and the approach of death. As we grow older we may become more vulnerable to attacks of despair in which our sense of the meaning and value of all that has gone before will seem to drain away. The Holy Spirit may compel us to deal with issues, doubts, and wounds that we avoided when we were more vigorous. Those challenges will prepare us further for our final surrender into the arms of God through our death. In all these struggles the grace of Christ will never fail us.

One of the hardest tests comes if the need for professional nursing means that a brother has to be cared for outside the community. This separation will call on the deepest resources of acceptance and trust in the brother who has to move away. All of us must do everything in our power to sustain his sense of connectedness with the community.

FORTY-EIGHT

Holy Death

The gospel proclaims that Christ has transformed death by his cross and resurrection and that through our Baptism we have already passed through death with him and have been incorporated into his risen body. But we grasp this mystery only by faith, accepting the inner struggle between doubt and confidence in Christ's promise of eternal life: "Very truly, I tell you, anyone who hears my word and believes him who sent me has eternal life, and does not come under judgment, but has passed from death to life." Day by day as we feed on Christ in the Eucharist our hope can be rekindled: "Those who eat my flesh and drink my blood have eternal life, and I will raise them up on the last day."

We are called to remember our mortality day by day with unflinching realism, shaking off the sleep of denial. Paradoxically, only those who remember that they are but dust, and to dust they shall return, are capable of accepting the presence of eternal life in each passing moment, and receiving ever fresh the good news of hope. The anticipation of death is essential if we are to live each day to the full as a precious gift, and rise to the urgency of our vocation as stewards who will be called to give account at Christ's coming. Remembering that death can come to us at any time will spur us to be prepared, by continual renewal of our repentance and acceptance of the forgiveness of God, to meet Christ without warning. We shall remember to express to one another those things that would make

us ready to part without regrets, especially thankfulness and reconciliation.

Week by week we are to accept every experience which requires
us to let go as an opportunity for Christ to bring us through death
into life. Hardships, renunciations, losses, bereavements, frustra-
tions, and risks are all ways in which death is at work in advance,
preparing us for the self-surrender of bodily death. Through them
we practice the final letting go of dying, so that it will be less strange
and terrifying to us.

In the community we shall experience the event of death in many
forms. A brother's death may be serene; other deaths will share in
the agony of Gethsemane or the physical and spiritual pain which
has tested many saints. Some of us will die filled with the light of
hope; others may enter the darkness of Jesus' dereliction. As brothers we will seek to uphold the one who is dying with compassion
and love, supporting him with prayer and the sacramental grace
that comes through Holy Communion and the Laying on of Hands
and Anointing.

The death of a brother may give rise to many varied feelings
among us which we can help one another to accept. We will not be
ashamed to grieve, as Christ grieved at the death of Lazarus, or to
show ourselves to be shaken. But Christ has prayed that those
whom God has given him will be with him where he is and will see
his glory. In our mourning and celebration of the liturgy of burial
we seek to show our trust that our brother is being brought into
the glory of God's presence. In Christ we are still one with our
departed brothers and we express this communion through regular
prayer for them and by recalling their lives on the anniversaries of
their deaths. We believe that they pray for us and that we will be
reunited when Christ gathers all creation to himself, so that God
may be all in all.

FORTY-NINE

The Hope of Glory

All praise and thanks be to the Father for the gift of the hope of glory. Through this gift the Holy Spirit opens all that we are and all that we do to the promise of eternal fulfillment beyond death.

In our prayer, in which we look to the glory of the ascended Christ and realize our union with him, we see only as "in a mirror, dimly"; the Spirit fills us with the hope of seeing him as he is, face to face. As we follow the way of conversion, and surrender to the grace which changes us from one degree of glory to another, our longing to be wholly transformed into his likeness deepens. Our own sufferings, and the pain we see in the world around us, sharpen our yearning for all creation "to be set free from its bondage to decay and...obtain the freedom of the glory of the children of God."

In our daily worship, hope stirs our desire to adore God for all eternity in the host of heaven. In the Eucharist we show forth Christ's death until his coming again, and the gift we receive in communion intensifies our expectation of that final coming. Inwardly we pray "Come, Lord Jesus," looking forward to that day when he will gather us for the eternal banquet that will unite all God's people in the joy of the Kingdom.

This gift of hope is woven into the texture of our daily life as a community. Living, working, and worshiping together as one body, calling nothing our own, we learn to anticipate the glory of the communion of saints, in which all joys are shared. The gift of hope is present whenever we minister to one another and to those whom God gives us to serve. Christ has promised that we shall bear fruit that lasts if we abide in him. Hope assures us that every act of witness, prayer, and service that draws others into the life of divine love builds up the eternal city of God.

In this hope we, the brothers of the Society of St. John the Evangelist, offer our whole life to the glory of God the Holy Trinity, thankful for the mercy that has drawn us into the divine life. Our hope lies not in what we have done for God, but in what God has done for us: "Every action by which his strength has been developed in us has been a deifying action, gathering us up into the participation of the divine nature, which is the blessed purpose of his incarnation, the fruit of his mediatorial love, the epiphany of his triumphant power."

Glory to the Father, and to the Son, and to the Holy Spirit: as it was in the beginning, is now, and will be for ever. Amen.

References

Except where noted, Fr. Richard Meux Benson is the author of all the published works cited.

Chapter 1: John 17:22,23; John 20:21

Chapter 2: John 1:18; John 21:22

Chapter 3: From an instruction on Readiness, 1874: p. 88, *Instructions on the Religious Life, Third Series* (London: Mowbray, 1951)

Chapter 4: 1 John 1:3; From an instruction on Life in Community, 1874: p. 81, *The Religious Vocation* (London: Mowbray, 1939)

Chapter 6: Phil. 2:6-8; Phil. 2:5; 2 Cor. 8:9; Eph. 3:19; John 1:16

Chapter 8: John 15:2; 2 Cor. 4:7; John 17:14; 1 Cor. 1:27,28

Chapter 9: Mark 10:30

Chapter 12: John 5:19,30

Chapter 16: *Opus dei*, the term used in the Rule of St. Benedict for the offering of corporate worship

Chapter 17: From an instruction on Communion, 1874: p. 157, *The Religious Vocation*

Chapter 18: From an instruction on the Divine Office, 1874: p. 166, *The Religious Vocation*

Chapter 19: Heb. 4:12; John 6:63; Eph. 4:15

Chapter 20: John 6:68

Chapter 21: 2 Pet. 1:4; John 14:23; Eph. 6:12; 1 Pet. 5:10,11

Chapter 23: 1 Cor. 12:4; Eph. 3:19; John 16:13,14; 2 Cor. 3:18

Chapter 24: *The Final Passover ii, pt 2* (London: Longmans, 1895), p. 307; Rom. 8:26,27; John 14:13; Evagrius of Pontus, *Chapters on Prayer,* chap. 124. (A modern translation by John Eudes Bamberger, OCSO is available: Evagrius Ponticus, *The Praktikos, Chapters on Prayer* [Spencer, Mass.: Cistercian Publications, 1970].); Rom. 8:21

Chapter 25: Instruction on Intercession, 1874: p. 108, *Instructions on the Religious Life, Third Series*

Chapter 26: Matt. 6:6; Ps. 132:14 RSV; John 12:24; *The Sayings of the Desert Fathers,* Abba Moses, no. 6

Chapter 29: Matt. 11:28

Chapter 30: From an instruction on Confession, 1874: p. 146, *The Religious Vocation*; John 14:6

Chapter 36: John 16:23

Chapter 38: Ps. 116:10-12 BCP

Chapter 39: John 10:18; 1 John 2:24

Chapter 41: Col. 1:16,17

Chapter 42: John 15:13-15; 2 Cor. 3:17

Chapter 43: John 15:12

Chapter 44: John 10:10; Ps. 139:13 BCP

Chapter 46: 2 Cor. 12:9; Col. 1:24; 2 Cor. 1:4

Chapter 48: John 5:24; John 6:54

Chapter 49: 1 Cor. 13:12; Rom. 8:21; Rev. 22:20; *The Name of Jesus,* a sermon preached before the University of Oxford on the 5th Sunday after Epiphany, 1865, by the Revd. R. M. Benson, MA, Student of Christ Church and Perpetual Curate of Cowley, Oxon. Rivington

Glossary

The Process of Creating
a New Rule of Life

The Rule as a Guide
to Personal Reflection

The Rule as a Guide for
Life in Community

Glossary

Advocate: the term used in John's gospel for the Holy Spirit, "Paraclete" in older translations of the New Testament. This term, favored by the church in which the fourth gospel was written, highlights the active role of the Spirit, defending, encouraging, and championing the community of believers.

Anglican Church: the word "Anglican" is derived from the Latin word for the English. The Anglican Communion is a fellowship of autonomous churches throughout the world that derive their origins through missionary work and migration from the Church of England, which became independent from the Roman Catholic Church in the sixteenth century. These churches are all connected by a common loyalty to the see of Canterbury. The Anglican Church in the USA is called the Episcopal Church, a name derived from the system of church order in which bishops are the leaders of the church.

Apostolic: a term deriving from the New Testament word "apostle," meaning "one who is sent." It is used in the Rule to refer to our vocation to active engagement in ministry and witness to the gospel.

Baptismal Renunciations: as part of the solemn covenant made in Baptism, the candidate renounces Satan and all the spiritual forces of wickedness that rebel against God, the evil powers of this world that corrupt and destroy the creatures of God, and all sinful desires that draw him or her from the love of God.

Canticles: these are portions of Scripture or religious texts appointed to be sung during the services that make up the Daily Office.

Celibacy: commitment to the permanent single state and sexual abstinence. Until recently the commitment was made in many religious orders under the form of a vow of chastity. However, it is common now to use the word chastity for the sexual integrity and fidelity that all Christians are committed to by their baptismal covenant.

Cell: the small private room in which a brother prays, sleeps, and studies in solitude.

Chanting: the singing of the psalms and canticles in simple repetitive melodies. There are varieties of styles in use, both ancient and modern. The Society makes extensive use of the historic chant style of western monasticism, known variously as plainsong, plain chant, or Gregorian chant.

Chapter: a formal assembly of the professed brothers of the community. The Superior presides and decisions made by the Chapter are binding on the whole community. In the Society of St. John the Evangelist the Chapter meets at least twice a year.

Clothing: during this ceremony, in which a postulant is admitted as a novice of the community, he puts on the habit of the Society for the first time.

Congregation: a regional subdivision of a religious order with its own Superior. In the Society of St. John the Evangelist there are two fully autonomous congregations, the English and the North American.

Daily Office: the sequence of liturgical services of prayer and praise appointed for the various times of the day. Some religious communities have their own distinctive forms of these services, following traditional or contemporary patterns. In the North American Congregation of the Society the Daily Office uses the patterns provided in *The Book of Common Prayer* of the Episcopal Church in the USA. Canadian houses of the Society would use the equivalent pattern provided by the Anglican Church in Canada.

Fellowship of St. John: is comprised of men and women in many walks of life who desire to live the Christian life in special association with the Society of St. John the Evangelist and who commit themselves to a simple rule of life. Most religious communities have similar associations or confraternities.

Formation: a traditional word used for the process of training through which a brother is initiated into the life and ministry of the community.

Greater Silence: the custom of refraining from conversations and all public activity between the last act of worship at night, the office of Compline, and the beginning of the working day the following morning. In practice this silence usually lasts from 9.20 pm to 9.00 am.

Habit: the form of the traditional monastic "uniform" used by the Society of St. John the Evangelist is a black double-breasted cassock over which a scapular is worn. A scapular is a long rectangle of material with an opening for the head, covering the front and back of the body. A thick black cord is wound three times round the waist and secured in a way that leaves both ends hanging down at the left side almost to the hem. The cord adopted at profession has three knots tied about six inches apart in one of the ends. These knots are reminders of the vows.

Liturgical Cycle: the succession of seasons and festivals in the Church's year, beginning with Advent and moving through Christmas, Epiphany, Lent, Eastertide, and Pentecost, through which the worshiping community renews its experience of the saving acts of God in Christ.

Monastic: this word is sometimes used to refer only to those historic orders that are primarily devoted to worship, asceticism, and prayer and whose members remain in stability in their monasteries, e.g. Benedictines, Carthusians, Cistercians. The Society of St. John the Evangelist is not a monastic community in this technical sense. The alternative usage that we follow in this Rule refers generally to the way of life common to all religious orders.

Poverty: the renunciation of personal property and the commitment to community of possessions. Before a brother can make this vow for life he must give away all his property to his family or any other persons or charitable causes, with the approval of the Superior. He may hand over his property to the common funds of the Society. Should a professed brother inherit property he must give it away. All gifts and earnings received by brothers are the common property of the community.

Reconciliation: the practice commonly known as "making one's confession." The Catechism of the Episcopal Church defines it in this way: "Reconciliation of a Penitent, or Penance, is the rite in which those who repent of their sins may confess them to God in the presence of a priest, and receive the assurance of pardon and the grace of absolution."

Reservation: the ancient practice of keeping portions of the consecrated bread and wine of the Eucharist in a fixed, locked container in a church where these signs of Christ's presence can be a focus of devotion as well as the source from which the sick and dying can receive Holy Communion.

Religious: a member of a religious order.

Retreat: the practice of withdrawing for a period of time from the normal routines of life in order to devote oneself to prayer and reflection.

Statutes: a collection of official regulations, drawn up by the Chapter and approved by the Visitor, that form the Society's constitution and lay down its formal procedures.

Superior: the elected leader of the Society. In the Society of St. John the Evangelist the Superior is elected by the Chapter for a term of three years. He is not allowed to serve more than three consecutive terms. In other communities the leader is also known by the titles Abbot or Prior.

Triune Life: an expression referring to the inner life of God as a Trinity of Persons, Father, Son, and Holy Spirit.

Visitor: religious communities elect a bishop of the Church to act as a Visitor, or Protector. It is his or her duty to check that the Superior and community are remaining faithful to their rule and statutes, to give advice when called upon, and to act as arbitrator if a serious dispute arises. In the Episcopal Church the Bishop Visitor has the authority to dissolve the religious vows of men and women who have been formally released from membership in a community.

Vows: the binding promises of poverty, celibacy, and obedience (or their equivalent in other religious orders).

The Process of Creating a New Rule of Life

An account of the process that our community used in creating its new Rule of life may be of interest to some readers, and offer useful suggestions for other religious communities or groups who are considering creating or revising a rule.

The community began in early 1988 by inviting a senior sister of the Religious of the Cenacle to lead us in discussion of the process of producing a new rule. She had played a leading role some years ago in the revision of the rule and constitutions of her order, an international order of women in the Roman Catholic Church whose primary mission is expressed in spiritual direction and formation and the leading of retreats. With her assistance we were able to draw up preliminary tables of the themes and subjects we wanted to see incorporated in our new Rule. She helped us to sketch out a process which would enable the community to bring its own theology, spirituality, and practice to consciousness and then progressively distill them into a written form.

So began our work, which we imagined would take us three or four years; in fact, we went on to spend eight years in the task. The process itself, we discovered, challenged the community to develop in many ways. We knew that the Rule would have to be an expression of complete consensus within the community. Just how extensive and deep the discussions would have to be for us to achieve a consensus in the expression of every aspect of our life was something we could discover only by experience. We made the decision at the beginning to include the novices of the community in all our discussions so that we could incorporate the insights of men coming new to our way of life.

The second stage of the process, lasting about two years, gave us a way to break up the ground and gain practice in discussion. The community was divided into small working groups to reflect on particular themes that would be taken up by the Rule, such as mission and ministry, worship, the three vows, authority and structure, tradition and ethos. When this initial work of exploration was completed, each group presented the findings to a gathering of the whole community and a provisional list of about thirty chapter headings was developed.

In the third stage of about six months a committee of four brothers, drawing on the notes of the working groups and other community discussions, produced brief guidelines for drafting a range of chapters. Br. Martin Smith was then appointed to begin writing actual chapters for the community to consider. We started with topics that seemed relatively uncontroversial and straightfor-ward so that we could gain confidence before moving on to the weightier sections.

In the fourth stage the community heard these draft chapters read in the course of our regular morning Chapter Office so we could begin to assimilate and reflect on them. The drafts were then subjected to criticism by the brothers in small groups and plenary sessions, most of which were held during our summer and winter gatherings when we were free from our normal responsibilities and ministries. After this first critique Br. Martin rewrote each chapter to incorporate the suggestions that arose in those discussions and then submitted it again for further criticism. Once it had reached a satisfactory form each chapter had regular use in the sequence of reading at the Chapter Office and in the formation of new members. Our growing familiarity with the new material enabled us to see where amplifications were necessary; topics were then subdivided and extra chapters drafted.

It was in these discussions that the hard work of the creation of the new Rule took place. Many of the topics that the Rule raised were ones that we had never before explored in depth together and ones about which we had done little sharing of our personal experience. We had to discover new resources of candor and trust when we were talking about such intimate matters as our prayer, sexuality, friendship, and experience of authority in the community. We had to find new levels of maturity to tackle subjects like the meaning of the vow of poverty where brothers had differing approaches. We discovered that it took time to establish the rhythms of discussion that enabled us eventually to give every sentence a form to which each brother could give assent.

It was especially during the final three years of the process that the community reaped the benefit of our growing maturity. We discovered the need to incorporate over a dozen new themes that we had not envisaged in the original sketch of the Rule, such as health and creativity, rest and recreation, and the graces of friendship. Our discussions about the significance of the Gospel of John in our life led us to a new appreciation of the figure of the disciple whom Jesus loved, on whose witness the gospel is based. We finally gained confidence to tackle the most challenging areas of life, in particular our mission and the vows of poverty, celibacy, and obedience, where the achievement of consensus was particularly demanding.

Before a final version was adopted the draft Rule was submitted to close scrutiny by twelve men and women outside the community.

They represented a variety of fields of expertise and included senior members of Anglican and Roman Catholic religious orders, writers, members of the Fellowship of St. John, theologians, leaders in the field of spirituality, psychologists, priests, bishops, and lay people. These readers submitted a large number of comments and suggestions that were collated and offered to the community for consideration. The draft Rule was then revised in the light of our discussion of their suggestions and submitted to the community for its final decisions. The Chapter met in September 1996 and formally adopted the Rule by a unanimous vote.

The Rule as a Guide to Personal Reflection

Since the early days of monasticism large numbers of Christians who follow the more usual paths of discipleship as single or married working people have found challenges and inspiration for their lives by meditating on the rules of religious orders. In the last ten years, for example, a number of books that explore ways in which contemporary lay men and women can discover profound guidance for their lives in the Rule of St. Benedict have become bestsellers. Here we provide some suggestions for ways to use the SSJE Rule as a resource for personal reflection on the Christian life.

If you dip into the Rule here and there you will soon discover that it is a very condensed and rich kind of text that does not lend itself to quick reading. Many insights are distilled into each page and to be assimilated these insights require a special kind of reading that is rather different from the usual method. Monastic rules call for the kind of reading that was given the name *lectio divina*, divine or holy reading, in the monastic tradition. This kind of reading takes things very slowly, and stops to ponder particular sentences and phrases in a leisurely way. It is reading that calls for gentle rumination on phrases and a patient expectation that hidden depths of meaning will emerge from praying with and around them. After surveying and dipping into the Rule you might want to choose one particular chapter and spend several sessions of meditation on it by reading slowly and dwelling on particular sentences and phrases that attract your attention. If it is your practice to devote regular times to meditation you might find that there is in some chapters material for six or seven sessions.

You may be bringing to your reading basic questions such as, What is prayer and meditation? What are we doing when we worship together? What does it mean to pray for others? If you are looking for insight into prayer and worship some chapters set out a rich fare of teaching and distill a whole tradition of spirituality. See, for example, the chapters "Worship," "The Eucharist," "The Mystery of Prayer," "Prayer and Life," "Meditative Prayer," "The Mystery of Intercession," and "The Practice of Intercession."

Other chapters offer springboards for reflection on a wide range of topics in Christian discipleship. Because this is the contemporary rule of a community that is actively engaged in the wider community you will discover many chapters whose teaching is applicable to your situation and may help you reflect on your response to the gospel. Chapters such as "Maintaining Our Health and Creativity" or "Rest and Recreation" do not need much translating. We are all alike in our need of encouragement to live creative, sane, and balanced lives responsive to the divine invitation to sabbath. You may wish to make your own notes on such chapters, spelling out the questions they raise for your own life.

The chapters that appear to be devoted to the particular disciplines of monastic life may seem less promising at first as sources of insight for your own life. However, their monastic perspective may prove helpful in casting light on unexplored dimensions of the Christian life. One example would be the chapter "Hospitality." While this deals with the responsibilities of the ministry of hospitality to which our Society is called, hospitality is a central theme in scriptural teaching about discipleship. The chapter could lead you to reflect on your own call to hospitality, the way you make others welcome in your home, the way you respond to strangers, the possibility that your practices of welcome and acceptance have a powerful spiritual dimension.

Two further examples would be the chapters "The Cell and Solitude" and "Silence." These chapters might raise questions for you to pursue such as, How much time do I allow myself to be alone to reckon with my own particular uniqueness and personhood? Do I allow myself to be so completely consumed by the claims of others that I lose touch with my own solitude and the axis of relationship with God on which my life really turns? Is my own private living space a place of prayer and meeting with God? Is there a place in my home where I can know what it is to be centered in God and seek his face? Am I allowing the overstimulus and bombardment of modern life to saturate my soul? Do I ever seek silence in which I can recover a sense of who I really am? Am I able to find an inner resource of silence that can help me let go of preoccupations, resentment, and the accumulating wear and tear of everyday pain?

Other examples of chapters which could fruitfully be the spring-board for reflection on discipleship include "Mutual Support and Encouragement," "The Maturing of Our Minds in Christ," "The Gifts and Challenges of Old Age," "Guidance and Reconciliation," and "Holy Death."

Contemporary spirituality is gradually becoming more faithful to the New Testament teaching that all baptized persons are called to ministry. The chapters "Mission and Service," "The Spirit of Mission and Service," and "Ministry in Practice" could be used as the basis for considering your own call to ministry, lay or ordained. They might stimulate a wide-ranging self-examination about the experience of being called to serve others, what your particular gift is, and the spirit in which you fulfill your ministry.

You may turn to the sections that deal with the vows of poverty, celibacy, and obedience with the assumption that these are the unique commitments that most clearly distinguish members of religious communities from their fellow Christians. However, those who take these vows would probably tell you that they do not experience these commitments as something exotic and specialized. We experience them as ways of wrestling with fundamental issues in our common human relationship to God. We all have to explore what it means to give ourselves, how we are to live our sexuality, and how we are to be responsive and responsible with others in Christian fellowship. The six chapters in the Rule on the vows may be approached not as windows into a uniquely specialized path of discipleship, but more as sources of reflection on some very fundamental realities of the gospel.

You may want to approach the chapters on poverty as an invitation to raise a whole range of questions about living the new life of the gospel set out in the Beatitudes. Pondering them may lead you to ask questions like these: What does it mean to believe in a self-giving God? What is my relationship with the poor? How do I give myself away? How do I express the sharing that is the hallmark of the new community formed by the Spirit? What value do I place on my own experience of limitation and brokenness?

Those living the single life may find much to apply directly to their lives in some of the reflections in the chapters on celibacy. But others who are living or seeking to live in marriage and partnership may find that these chapters act as a foil for reflection on their own way of sexual intimacy, and provoke some fundamental questions: Do I experience God personally calling and shaping my life in the way I am living out my sexuality? With what kind of respect and reverence do I engage with other people? How is my inner drive toward intimacy and my sexuality related to God's love for me and desire for union with me? How do I support other people in their intimate relationships? How do I find the courage to face the inner loneliness that is intrinsic to my human identity?

The chapters on obedience and life in community raise issues of power and accountability that all of us are called to reckon with: How do I use my power, my voice? How do I cooperate with others to make community and bring about creative developments of the gifts God has given us? Do I dominate or do I repress myself? To whom am I accountable? Where do I put my allegiance and invest my loyalty? Is individualism my ideal or have I grasped the mystery of living as a member of the Body of Christ, caught up in the interaction and interdependence of God's way of life? How do I play my part with a full confidence in the gifts God has given me? How do I outgrow the immature need to have things go my way?

Another way of reading the Rule is to bring to it your own questions about God. The way of life that the Rule guides and interprets is a life of seeking and responding to God. You may want to read each chapter with the questions: What is this chapter saying about God? What does it say about Christ and the Holy Spirit? Am I drawn to the God spoken of in these pages?

A spiritual practice with deep roots and a close connection with monastic life is that of creating a personal rule of life. For a community the rule of life is not a rigid law that makes daily life into the working of a machine. Rather, it is a kind of constitution or bill of rights that makes sure that all the different elements of a Spirit-filled life in Christ are valued and given their due place in the whole. A rule recognizes that we are subject to all sorts of pressures that work to make life one-sided, and repress essential aspects of our calling.

Each individual is in some way a miniature community, subject to internal and external pressures to avoid or neglect some aspect of her or his wholeness as a member of Christ. So it is the practice of many serious Christians to make a covenant with themselves, a pattern of practice and discipline to which they commit themselves to live in as full and balanced a way as possible. This personal rule of life is not a rigid law but a constitution that helps hold together the many elements of the whole self.

Studying the SSJE Rule of life might prove to be a valuable stimulus for some readers to enhance or create a personal rule of life by setting out a wide range of issues that call for attention and commitment. One way of using the Rule may be to survey the whole Rule and list the kind of questions of commitment it raises, questions such as: How shall I commit myself to regular prayer and worship? How shall I feed on the scriptures regularly? How often should I go on retreat? How shall I express my commitment to ministry? What kind of discipline should I adopt to make sure that I keep learning and growing as a Christian through reading and study? A personal rule of life can be valuable even in its simplest form. It gives strength to that inner part of ourselves that wants to resist scatteredness and haphazardness in our lives. It can reinforce the dignity that comes with commitment.

Some readers may discover an inner sense of identification and empathy with the monastic way. From the very beginning of this movement in the church there have been many who are not called actually to belong to a religious community but who have a deep sense of sharing in the monastic spirit and values. This is the phenomenon of "interiorized monasticism," to use a phrase of the Eastern Church. You may discover that you want to use this Rule as a resource in drawing up a substantial personal rule of life that expresses this inner identification. Or regular reading of it may act as a constant encouragement to live monastic values in the context of your everyday life.

The Rule as a Guide for Life in Community

To be a Christian is to be a member of the Body of Christ and Christian life can only be experienced in a community. The most familiar expression of this common life is the parish, but it is not the only one. There are other ways in which Christians form community in order to experience and express the *koinonia*, the fellowship, of the Holy Spirit. Christians come together in various kinds of societies, groups, teams, households, and organizations in order to bring focus to their life of ministry or discipleship and give one another mutual support.

The formation of community is difficult in the modern world; life is mobile, fractured, pressured. We have become aware of the psychological complexity of any group. The experience of true community is richly rewarding, all the more so because of the fragmentation and isolation that are so prevalent in our society. But many resources of wisdom are needed for communities not only to last, but to flourish. In the past the rules of religious orders have been one of those resources from which other kinds of Christian societies, households, and groups have drawn inspiration. Can they provide a resource today?

We offer our Rule for public reflection so that other Christian groups might find it a stimulus and resource as they consider their corporate mission and way of life. A rule of life is basically an articulation, a breaking into the open light of consciousness, of values, practices, habits, and conceptions that would otherwise remain tacit, taken for granted. As long as these things are unconscious in the life of a group, their power and reality is obscured and muffled. Once identified, named, owned, and celebrated their latent energy is released. We might put it this way: every group already has, in one sense, a rule of life—its values and ways of doing things. The challenge is to identify and to authenticate what they are. A group can become a truer expression of community when it is able to express its own tacit rule. There are several ways the SSJE Rule of life might be a helpful example in this process of taking conscious responsibility for the dynamics and values of a community.

It is widely recognized that every form of community or group should be able to articulate a mission statement that summarizes its purpose. But mission statements have the limitations that come with brevity. It has been said that "God is in the details" and often a community needs to go beyond the generalities of a mission statement if it is truly to understand its life. The SSJE Rule of life might be a valuable resource for a group that wants to take the next step to a fuller articulation of its life.

Group study of the Rule, especially those chapters that directly deal with life in community, might enable the members to identify a series of essential questions that they need to address. Some of the questions will be along these lines: What do we believe about the initiative and call of God in the formation of our group? What does God desire of us? What draws us to belong? What can we be together that we cannot be as individuals? What are the criteria for new members to be admitted? How do we take responsibility for initiating them? How do we deal with members leaving? How is power and authority distributed? What is our witness? How are we called to minister? What is the special orientation or spirituality of the group that makes us unique? What particular values are central to our identity? What are the fundamental disciplines we commit ourselves to, as distinct from the things that are personal options? What is the place of worship in our lives?

It is intriguing to imagine a representative team of members of a parish giving themselves the challenge of drawing up a parish rule of life that parallels the rule of a religious order and uses it as a basic model. Of course, many parishes have gone a long way in producing written materials that express the life of the community in an ample way. But it would be a further step to pull this self-description together into a rule. We might imagine this team exploring and expressing the particular dedication and tradition of the parish; the values it holds up as a witnessing community; the commitments that belong to dedicated membership; the articulation of its mission and ministry and the spirit in which those are expressed; its pattern of worship and spirituality; its plan for initiating new members and training them in ministry; its values about personal relationships and its covenant with employees; its special regard for children and the aged; its practices and values around leadership, authority, and shared decision-making; its practice in respect to divisions and the need for reconciliation.

It is also our hope that smaller teams of people working together in ministry might discover from joint reflection on this Rule of life some unexplored potential in their life together. It might be as simple as the realization that a deeper unity and cohesion may be found not through self-conscious processing of personal issues but from commitment to shared times of meditation, and worship together in the Daily Office. Or reading the Rule might be an incentive to identifying and expressing the shared vision of the group so that it can move beyond the issue of personal cooperation to that of a common spirituality.

Our experience in the Society of St. John the Evangelist suggests that the process of creating a rule of life, though very demanding, is extraordinarily rewarding. We in the religious life would be fascinated and excited by the prospect of seeing how other expressions of Christian community could generate rules that parallel our own.